Martin Murphy

MARTIN MURPHY JR.
California Pioneer 1844-1884

SISTER GABRIELLE SULLIVAN

Sister Gabrielle Sullivan
S.N.J.de N.

PACIFIC CENTER FOR WESTERN HISTORICAL STUDIES
UNIVERSITY OF THE PACIFIC, STOCKTON, CALIF. 95204

PACIFIC CENTER FOR WESTERN HISTORICAL STUDIES
Monograph Number Four

FIRST EDITION
PRINTED IN THE U.S.A.

TABLE OF CONTENTS

PREFACE

Martin Murphy, Jr., holds a place in the *Chronicles of the Builders of the Commonwealth* which was published by Hubert Howe Bancroft. To preserve the accounts of men regarded as key figures in the development of California, Bancroft selected mainly self-made men who were known for their industry and public spirit as builders of the American West. He included Martin Murphy, Jr., an immigrant from Ireland in the first half of the nineteenth century who became a notable business man and philanthropist of Santa Clara Valley in the second half of the century.

Two landmarks erected in tribute to him, one in Sacramento County and one in Santa Clara County, attest to prestige once enjoyed. They suggest that a man who had earned such memorials might deserve a more elaborate treatment than what was feasible within the purpose of the Bancroft *Chronicles*. Since bibliographical tools down to 1962 did not list any item readily associated with him outside the pages of Bancroft, the present work was undertaken.

A man who is memorialized in two landmarks in locales one hundred and fifty miles apart may be assumed to have had some impact on his times and that there would be readily available source material for his biography. The opposite proved to be the case. There were no sources available in the usual repositories or apparently elsewhere. The effort to resolve the paradox between the obvious one-time prominence of the man and the current poverty of materials finally resulted in an explanation by a member of the Murphy family that a "trunk of Murphy papers" had once existed, but that its whereabouts was now unknown. Another descendant of Martin Murphy, Jr., suggested that the trunk with its contents might have been auctioned off. After a three-year search, the vanished trunk, located in the storeroom of a San Francisco auction house, Butterfield and Butterfield, was given to me. I herewith gratefully acknowledge the generosity of this firm, represented by the manager, Mr. George Morf, in giving the trunk to me.

The contents of the trunk may be summarized as follows:

the indenture for the sale of his first rancho in the Sacramento Valley
for $50,000 and other indentures;
copies of land grants and maps;
city and county tax receipts which helped to establish ownership and
value of property;
numerous promissary notes;
Martin Murphy's certificate of citizenship dated November 1, 1855; and
congratulatory letters to Mr. and Mrs. Murphy on the occasion of their
Golden Jubilee.

All is primary material; some of it substantiates what is found in
Bancroft and in other authors, but much of it has not been used
hitherto. One highly instructive item is an indenture dated January
17, 1851 which tells of a dangerous journey Martin Murphy was
about to take and of the transfer of ownership of all his posses-
sions to his wife Mary. There is no signature, but the document
bears Martin Murphy's "mark" — a cross. This clears up the mys-
tery of why the letters and memoranda on which historians rely
so heavily are not available in the case of this pioneer. I conclude
from examining the materials in the trunk that Mr. Murphy could
not write. (See Appendix 6.)

The first of the sources used for this paper was the Dictation
made to Alfred Bates by Bernard D. Murphy concerning his father
Martin Murphy, Jr. The Dictation is a summary of facts related to
the Murphy family from its origin in County Wexford, Ireland,
to their residence in the Santa Clara Valley. The information given
to Alfred Bates, an employee of Hubert Howe Bancroft, was the
basis for the biographical account of Murphy in the *Chronicles of
the Builders of the Commonwealth*. Other primary material has
made it possible to indicate what material available was used by
Bancroft and the pressures put upon him by an interested lawyer.
(See Appendix 5.)

The scope of this study extends from Martin Murphy's emigration from Ireland through his several choices of homesite to the
final phase of his life on his rancho Pastoria de las Borregas. The
historical background of his time facilitates an understanding of
Murphy's life and character as he moved from his home in County
Wexford, Ireland, to Canada, Missouri, and California. After six
years in Sacramento, he settled in 1850 in the Santa Clara Valley
where for thirty-four years he spent his energy developing his
rancho which later became the site of Sunnyvale, and in building
up the city of San Jose.

The writer wishes to express her sincere gratitude to the Right

Reverend James M. Campbell, Dean of the Pacific Coast Branch of the Catholic University of America, for his continued interest and encouragement. A special note of thanks is due to the late Professor John T. Farrell of Catholic University who, as the Major Professor appointed for the dissertation, gave essential encouragement at a time when it seemed that nothing would come of the project because of the state of the evidence originally uncovered. Gratitude is expressed to Sister Gertrude Mary Gray of the College of the Holy Names under whose careful guidance the work was completed and to Reverend Aubert J. Clark, O.F.M Conv., Associate Professor at Catholic University, who acted as reader. Grateful appreciation is extended to Sister Paula Brizzolara, former Provincial Superior of the California Sisters of Notre Dame, for suggesting this topic as her contribution to Californiana and her sustained interest in its progress. Likewise to my sister Clotilde for her unflagging interest and assistance in the collection of source material. The valuable assistance rendered by the following descendants of the Martin Murphy, Jr. family is gratefully acknowledged: Mr. Irvin Frasse, Miss Muriel Wright, Mrs. Frank R. Stockton, Mrs. Ann Derby Tipton, Mrs. Gerald D. Kennedy, Mrs. I. H. Polk. Gratitude is expressed for the information supplied by Mr. Clyde Arbuckle and Mr. Theron Fox of the California Landmarks Commission, Mr. Reginald R. Stuart of the California Historical Foundation at the University of the Pacific, Reverend Arthur D. Spearman, Archivist of the University of Santa Clara, Reverend Wilfred Schoenberg of Gonzaga University, Reverend Augustin C. Ward of St. Stanislaus Seminary, Florissant, Missouri, Reverend Raymond Kennedy, St. Martin's Rectory, Sunnyvale, Reverend Charles N. McCarthy, O.S.A., New Ross, Ireland, Mrs. Mary West of the Sunnyvale Historical Society, Mr. Richard Barrett of the *San Jose Mercury*, and Mr. Francis Corbett who is an authority on the California Land Grants. Likewise a debt of gratitude is acknowledged to Mr. Allan R. Ottley and staff of the California State Library, also to the librarians and staffs of the Bancroft Library at the University of California and the University of San Francisco for their friendly and beneficial assistance.

INTRODUCTION

Martin Murphy, Jr. was born in 1807 into a world in transition during the European war caused by the French Revolution. Napolean had just completed the series of victories of Austerlitz, Jena, and Friedland that brought him near the height of his power when he signed the Peace of Tilsit in 1807 with Tsar Alexander I of Russia. The previous year the nine-century-old Holy Roman Empire had come to an end since the Hapsburg Emperor Francis had been forced to reduce his title to Emperor of Austria. England, in the forty-seventh year of the reign of George III, was facing the fourteenth year of war against France without the leadership of William Pitt.

By the time Martin Murphy entered his teens in 1820, a new era had begun. The Bourbons in the person of Louis XVIII had been restored to the throne of France after the defeat of Napoleon in 1815. Prince Metternich, Chancellor of Austria, dominated the policy of the European nations through the Concert of Europe in order to maintain the status quo established by the Congress of Vienna. In 1820 King George IV began his reign of ten years, a decade of momentous change in England. The Bourbon king, Ferdinand VII, had returned to the throne of Spain, but a Spain that no longer controlled a great empire in America. In the United States, which had doubled in size by the Louisiana Purchase, the year 1820 was marked by the Missouri Compromise which gave a temporary solution to the problem of slavery in relation to westward expansion.

Great Britain, though a great power in world politics, had to solve grave internal problems in the British Isles and the Empire. Three major issues disturbed domestic peace in England: representation in Parliament, civic rights for disfranchised Catholics, and labor agitation growing out of the economic changes resulting from the industrial revolution of the eighteenth century. In the decade of the 1820's the only problem settled was that of Catholic Emancipation, driven through Parliament by the Duke of Wellington in 1829 to avoid civil war. Labor conditions reached a crisis

I

at the time of the Peterloo Massacre in 1819, and in 1825 secured the repeal of the Combination Law which had forbidden the union of workers. Definite improvement, however, came only in the next decade with the Factory Act of 1833.

Martin Murphy grew up in an Ireland that was adjusting to a new political situation. The Act of Union in 1800 had closed the Irish Parliament in Dublin and opened the British Parliament in Westminster to representatives from Ireland in the Lords and the Commons. Though Catholics represented three-fourths of the four million in 1800, political control remained in the hands of the Protestant Anglo-Irish group and no Catholic could be elected to Parliament. In 1823 Daniel O'Connell formed the Catholic Association which organized the forty-shilling freeholders to support Catholic candidates against the Anglo-Irish incumbents. Five years later O'Connell won the Parliamentary election in Clare against Vesey Fitzgerald, forced attention on the required oath for his seat, and won finally not only his place in the House of Commons, but also Catholic Emancipation for the United Kingdom in 1829.

The union of 1800 failed to bring peaceful prosperity to the Irish and in the post-war years the social and economic conditions in Ireland contained every element for the production of national agitation. The country was subject to the exactions of an alien church, absentee landlords, and political-religious animosities. Wealth was concentrated in the hands of a few; a third of the population verged on starvation. Though some economic restrictions on trade had been removed, Ireland depended on linen industries and agriculture as her main supports. The industrial revolution which had increased unemployment in the British Isles stimulated emigration. By the second decade of the century emigration to the British colonies or the United States seemed the sole avenue of escape from economic problems and loss of freedom.

In 1820 the first members of the Murphy family emigrated to Canada. Eight years later, Martin Murphy and his sister Margaret joined them in Quebec. They found that ideal conditions did not exist in Quebec, for in some respects the political situation bore similarity to that of Ireland. In the 1830's Canadians struggled to achieve self-government. Oligarchies representing a wealthy pro-British group in Upper Canada gained preponderant control, and minimized the French Catholic group in Lower Canada. The British government, in spite of periodic efforts at compromise and moderation, favored the English settlers. By the 1830's there had arisen a demand for government more responsive to the popular will. The success of the Parliamentary reform in Britain in 1832

II

was a further encouragement to reform sentiment in Canada where many of the recent immigrants from the British Isles had already been influenced by liberalism in the country they had left.

The Murphy family merged successfully with the French settlers near Quebec, but it was in this area of Lower Canada that strife of rival tendencies broke into open revolt in 1837. The British Parliament suspended the constitution of Lower Canada and the Crown appointed John Lambton, Earl of Durham, to find a remedy. His part in Parliamentary reform and his liberal views made him acceptable to the Canadians and his famous Report marked the beginning of a transition in Canada which led to Dominion status in 1867. Early in the 1840's, however, the Murphy families decided to leave Quebec and to settle in Missouri, considering that the United States provided a working example of popular sovereignty and economic prosperity.

The Murphys came to Missouri when it was the frontier of the nation on the rim of an unformed region abounding in natural resources and attracting settlers, particularly to Oregon and California. Though California belonged to Mexico, the mountain men and the fur traders had publicized the attractions of the region. In 1841 John Bidwell proved that an overland journey could be made successfully by emigrants who wished to settle in California. Already there were Americans who had come by sea as traders, settled there, married Mexican women, and as citizens of Mexico received large grants of land to be used as ranchos for cattle.

When Martin Murphy considered California, he contemplated a culture quite different from the ones he had so far experienced. California had been an almost autonomous province of Mexico since 1821; the Missions had declined since their secularization in 1834, and the extensive ranchos dominated California life through the hide and tallow trade with English and American ships.

The Martin Murphys came overland to California in 1844 to find the Mexican government unstable, and to face within a few years the transfer of the region to the United States, the Gold Rush, and the establishment of the government of the state of California. By 1850 Martin Murphy, Jr. had moved from the Sacramento mining region to the rich agricultural valley of Santa Clara. There for almost four decades he utilized the experiences of his varied life and his natural talents to building a new community in California.

Spain had granted land to retired soldiers and settlers, but the majority of land grants were made during the Mexican period. Foreigners received grants as well as the Spanish-speaking natives, provided they met the requirements of California law. Prior to 1848 there was no accurate survey of the great grants in existence and boundary marks which had been set up were usually inaccurate and often temporary in character.

The Treaty of Guadalupe-Hidalgo in 1848 by which Mexico ceded California to the United States made provision that private ownership agreements which had been made between the Mexican government and its subjects would be respected by the United States. After 1848, when California came under the sovereignty of the United States, the official survey designated all vacant, unappropriated, and unreserved land as "Public Lands;" lands that had been granted under Spanish or Mexican sovereignty as "Private Grants."

Unsettled political conditions prevailed in the ceded territory at this time while the Gold Rush of 1849 increased the American and European Immigration into California. The population increase, though effecting California's immediate statehood in 1850, also aggravated the "squatter problem" and the resulting conflict of land claims.

The year following California's entrance into the Union, an Act of Congress, March 3, 1851, created a Board of Land Commissioners to operate within the framework of the General Land Office in Washington, D.C. The Board located itself in the San Francisco office of the United States Surveyor General of California. This Board's instructions were to ascertain the rightful claimants of grants and to determine the extent of each of the ranchos involved. Through this local land office the numerous Murphy ranchos came under scrutiny and all were ultimately verified.

CHAPTER I

WEXFORD, QUEBEC, AND MISSOURI

The family of Martin Murphy, Sr. resided at Balnamough near the town of Wexford, Ireland, at the opening of the nineteenth century.[1] Martin married Mary Foley and a number of children were born to them at Balnamough. The oldest son was Martin, Jr., born November 9, 1807.[2] In the years before the family left Ireland, two other sons were born, James and Bernard, and three daughters, Margaret, Joanna, and Mary.[3] The time of Martin, Jr.'s birth was a period of stress in Ireland. To understand the fiber and spirit of this Catholic pioneer, the conditions in Wexford in the early nineteenth century must be considered so that the forces which motivated emigration from the homeland may be understood.

Wexford was a small town approximately a mile in extent from north to south and situated on the River Slaney. This maritime town, associated with the earliest records of Irish history, was a favorite place for effecting a landing on the island.[4] Originally Wexford was a Danish settlement; later it drew settlers from England and the continent. Towards the end of the eighteenth century Wexford was a pronounced English enclave, but up to the rebellion of 1798 the Irish and English residents enjoyed amicable relations.[5]

Although Wexford was the focus of the Rebellion of 1798, the area had been tranquil before the outbreak and the people were least imbued with the nationalism of the United Irish Association.[6] The British authorities had won the people's support and confidence; efforts of the Association to incite an insurrection had failed. While property holders in Wexford were aware that a rebellion would be dangerous to their interests, nevertheless the groups that ultimately participated in the uprising included cottiers, farm laborers, and discontented farm owners.[7] Though peace was restored after 1798, the people of Wexford were still helpless and oppressed.

The hard conditions which followed in the wake of the rebellion were relieved somewhat by the current struggles against Napoleon which brought higher prices for Irish agricultural products. Those of the farmers who were industrious surmounted the handicaps of poor soil and high rents sufficiently to pay their rents and make some profits.[8] The greatest concentration of Ireland's wheat production at this time was in the sunny corner of County Wexford.[9] Here the families prospered until the overthrow of Napoleon in 1815, when the Irish producer was driven out of the English market and the problem of landholding again occupied the center of the stage. A depression struck the agricultural interests in the south of Ireland between 1815 and 1826 so that in this period many farmers emigrated from Ireland to America[10]

Martin Murphy, Sr. was the holder of a fair-sized farm by Irish standards. He was able to provide a decent livelihood for his family and some measure of prosperity as long as the war years kept up the price of his produce. Into this temporarily happy situation Martin Jr. was born in 1807. But the economic well-being which his father's industry won for his children would not be extended in the Ireland of that day to the field of education.

Practically nothing can be ascertained specifically about the education of Martin, Jr.; but, as a general rule, Catholic boys had difficulty in securing an education. English and Anglo-Irish statesmen had long endeavored to Protestantize Ireland by controlling education. Charter schools supported by the state and proselytizing in character had been established as early as 1733. Catholic parents avoided enrolling their children in these institutions because they feared they might lose their Catholic faith.[11]

Under the Penal Laws of Ireland the laity were no better off than the clergy in the matter of civil rights. The laws affecting education were intended to reduce Catholics to a condition of extreme ignorance. Catholics were excluded from the university; a Catholic could be penalized for tutoring or opening a school.[12] By law, the Irish were denied a European education, hence the only alternative to the charter schools was a type of school brought into existence by sheer necessity known as the hedge-school.[13] By 1794 most of the more serious grievances of the Irish lay Catholics relating to education were removed;[14] but, until about 1817 Roman Catholic children continued to remain in most instances "without any other instruction than such as they could obtain in that ordinary class of country pay schools, generally known in Ireland by the name of hedge-schools."[15]

Irish impoverishment in the nineteenth century as a result of the Penal Laws prevented intellectual advancement. Existing conditions made the planning of an effective system of primary education impossible, and, until the national school system came into practice in 1831, the Irish had to rely on hedge-schools.[16]

Whatever formal education Martin Murphy had as a child would have been under the conditions described and, consequently, on a very limited scale. There is ample evidence that he could not write.[17] These deprivations of his youth were to bear fruit years later in his devotion to the cause of learning and his willingness to give financial assistance to educational institutions.[18]

Throughout the years of persecution in Ireland, the aim of Protestant legislators was to make the Catholic population powerless and poor. The Penal Laws succeeded in the exclusion of Catholics from Parliament, from legal professions, and from all civil offices. Catholics did become helpless, lacking the strength to rebel, the hope of redress, or even the courage to complain; but they remained Catholic.

The religious training of Catholic children was not a part of the educational system in Ireland. Though the parish priest was tolerated, the work he could accomplish was limited by government regulations which denied him the assistance of a curate.[19] Seminaries, which elsewhere served as educational centers, did not exist in Ireland. In view of the limited number of priests and the Protestant Charter Schools, the major part of the task of teaching religion fell upon Catholic parents. The Murphy home, like other Irish Catholic homes, became the stronghold for all the basic training in the Faith. Martin Murphy Jr.'s heritage of strong Catholicity was preserved by him and perpetuated by members of his family. His later efforts to establish a satisfactory homestead in California were motivated by the desire to provide the two important aspects of life, namely, religion and education, for his sons and daughters.[20]

By 1820 the adverse conditions in Wexford under which the family was living led Martin Murphy, Sr. to leave his farm and to set out for Canada with his wife and four of his six children.[21] When he arrived in Canada he purchased land and settled in the small town of Frampton, southeast of Quebec.[22]

Eight years elapsed before Martin and his sister Margaret joined the family in the New World. On April 9, 1828, Martin, aged twenty-one, and his seventeen-year-old sister Margaret left Ireland for Canada.[23] Wexford, the point of embarcation, was an emigrant port and in the past years had sent several ships to Quebec. The travelers were registered aboard the *Thomas Farrell,* one of the packet ships which plied between Wexford and Quebec. When three days out, damage from rough weather compelled them to return to Waterford harbor. Two weeks' delay for repairs also decreased the passenger list; many less valiant than the Murphys changed their plans and abandoned the voyage.[24] After the

3

Thomas Farrell was made seaworthy, they made a comparatively short twenty-eight-day trip across the Atlantic.[25]

On arrival in Quebec, Margaret joined the family at Frampton. Martin, Jr. remained in the city of Quebec where he engaged in selling merchandise for a while. To an Irish farmer, business of this kind was uncongenial and he yearned for the rural life and the possession of his own land. Despite the difficulties which are endemic in pioneer living the young man persevered with courage and industry.

Meanwhile another matter occupied Martin's attention while in Quebec. He renewed acquaintance with the Bolger family, friends from Ireland whose land had been adjacent to that of his father. The details are lacking for the courtship of Martin Murphy and Mary Bolger, but records show that they were married by Father McMahon in the French Cathedral of Quebec, July 18, 1831.[26]

The first years of their married life were spent in Quebec. After an epidemic of cholera caused the death of two of their children, Mary and Nellie, living in that city seemed inadvisable. New agricultural sections were under development and land was available. Martin purchased two hundred acres near Frampton, the area where twelve years before his father had organized Irish settlers among the French Canadians.[27] The forested land was hard to clear, but Martin acquired the frontier skills necessary for survival; he went to work felling trees, shaping planks, and built a home for his wife and the four sons born in Canada.[28]

Emigration from Lower Canada to the United States was noticeable as early as 1806 when Canadians discovered the higher wages paid there and many immigrants soon became settled residents in the eastern states.[29] Martin Murphy, Sr. considered moving across the border in 1840 in view of the many influential factors. Canadian political unrest centered about the agitation for self-government since the colonial administration had proved inadequate. Farmers found difficulty with transportation of produce owing to lack of roads. and the impassability of the St. Lawrence River five months of the year.[30] Decline in wheat prices, crop failures in 1836 and 1837, and the financial panic and depression of 1837 made many people in Canada literally desperate.[31] Reports from the United States of rapid settlement and economic progress had an effect on the movement of population from Canada across the border. Living under the more democratic conditions of American institutions was attractive; also land was cheap. Martin Murphy, Sr. responded to the encouraging reports from the United States and left Canada in 1840.[32]

4

Though the union of Upper and Lower Canada was realized in 1841, the political situation was unsatisfactory. A theme that persisted was the contrasting of the economic conditions in Canada with those prevalent in the United States. Brighter prospects to the south caused a considerable number of immigrants who arrived in Quebec to continue their journey south. Martin, Jr. was susceptible to these and other influences which drew him across the border. The sterile soil and harsh climate of eastern Canada were serious drawbacks to protracted settlement and he was determined to move to a more hospitable region.[33] There were glowing reports about the resources of Missouri.[34] A second instance of parental influence, therefore, now appears in the Murphy story when in September of 1842 Martin followed his father to Missouri.[35]

Though means of water travel had improved by the 1840's, the journey was still long and arduous.

From Quebec they steamed up the St. Lawrence to Montreal; thence across Lake St. Louis; from here once more on the bosom of the mighty river to Kingston; again across Lake Ontario; up the Niagara River to Lewiston just below the Falls; from Lewiston to Buffalo, across Lake Erie to Cleveland, Ohio; there by canal to Portsmouth on the Ohio River; from here by steamer to Cincinnati, whence they proceeded to Louisville, Kentucky; thence down the Ohio to Cairo, and traveling on the Mississippi, the "father of waters" to St. Louis.[36]

From the city of St. Louis, Martin Murphy followed the Missouri River up to the Platte Purchase,[37] south of the city of St. Joseph.[38] Here he purchased 320 acres near his father's land in Holt County,[39] a fertile area east of the Missouri River and southeast of its tributary the Platte River. With the asset of farming experience gained in Wexford and Quebec, Martin Murphy set himself to the cultivation of corn and wheat.[40]

But Missouri proved to be only a brief pause on the way to California. The water courses of the area made the soil richly productive, but the region had disadvantages at that time which led many hopeful settlers ultimately to move on. One of these drawbacks was the malarial climate. Another was the lack of educational opportunities. A third, for Catholic families like the Murphys, was the remoteness from organized Catholicism. Stories about contrasting advantages in Oregon and California by persons who claimed to have visited these territories appealed to the more venturesome and resolute quite apart from misgivings about local conditions. The equivalent of a publicity campaign in behalf of the Far West was under way in the Platte River country of the Missouri in the 1840's, all the more effective because it was not a planned campaign.

Malaria struck the Murphys cruelly in 1843. Mary, the wife of Martin Murphy, Sr., and Martin, Jr.'s six-month-old daughter Ann Elizabeth died of it.[41] At this critical juncture, the Jesuit Father Christian Hoecken came to minister to the afflicted and to comfort the family in sorrow.[42] In his visits to the Murphys, Father Hoecken helped to determine their future by his reports on California.[43] To other arguments in its favor, he added the decisive factor that Catholicism was the established religion in this Mexican-governed territory. With renewed hopes of the benefits of religion, educational opportunity, and agricultural success which California promised, the Murphys resolved on another overland migration.

THE MURPHY PARTY, From a Painting by Andrew P. Hill, representing the first emigrant party ascending to the Summit from Donner Lake, in October, 1844.

CHAPTER II

OVERLAND TO CALIFORNIA IN 1844

The Missouri valley was a region of the fur trade from the eighteenth century into the first half of the nineteenth century until the time of westward emigration set in about 1843[1] The city of St. Louis formed the principal center for commerce in furs[2] and the surrounding area became the focus for much of the emigration activity as well as a place where news of the far west circulated among trappers, traders, and possible settlers.

The first of the organized parties to start for California originated in Platte County,[3] Missouri, where the Western Emigration Society enlisted recruits for overland passage and provided a systematic program for the expedition.[4] As far as can be determined, the Murphys in 1844 were not recruited by any society but organized and financed their own party.[5] The seemingly impossible conquest of the plains challenged the Murphys as it had all of the pioneers going to California in the 1840's.

In the spring of 1844, the elder Murphy, then in his fifty-ninth year, and Martin, Jr., thirty-seven, disposed of their farms,[6] purchased oxen, wagons, and provisions and made ready to leave Missouri.[7] They journeyed from the Platte Purchase south of St. Joseph to the rendezvous at Council Bluffs in southwest Iowa where another band of emigrants bound for Oregon was waiting. A few days were spent here making repairs and perfecting the organization of the wagon train. There were natural candidates for leadership in both the Murphy family and in the group of people bound for Oregon; domination by one group would have alienated the other.[8] The Martin Murphys were undoubtedly key figures among the men; but, lacking western experience, they could not initiate plans.[9] Diplomacy and democracy of the frontier exerted their influence and the choice for captaincy fell upon Elisha Stevens.[10] The Murphy assembly, smaller than the Oregon-bound group, consisted of about fifty persons distributed in eleven wagons.[11]

The date of departure from Council Bluffs was set for May 18, 1844.[12] The personnel of the Murphy party was excellent having people of general good sense, necessary practical ability, and extensive western experience.[13] A harmonious spirit prevented disputes among the members of the caravan, and a friendly attitude toward the Indians averted trouble as they approached the Fort Laramie area where approximately four thousand Sioux were encamped.[14]

Anyone starting for California in 1844 had a built-in insurance that he could get through to Oregon if he changed his mind at Fort Hall.[15] Fort Hall occupied a strategic position on the route of travel from Missouri to the coast. Here the trail to the Pacific divided, one branch leading on to Oregon, the other to California. The Oregon company took the north-western route;[16] those bound for California, the southwestern branch, a fairly well-defined trail to the headwaters of the Humboldt River.[17] Careful management and the good leadership of Elisha Stevens brought the party safely and in remarkably good condition to the Humboldt Sink in western Nevada by October 24, 1844.[18]

As far as evidence goes, the men of the Stevens-Murphy party had little certain knowledge of what lay west of the Humboldt Sink and they held consultations to decide on either a southerly route or one directly west. They met an old Indian whom they named Truckee.[19] He talked with Caleb Greenwood by means of signs and diagrams drawn on the ground. From him it was learned that fifty or sixty miles to the west there was a river that flowed easterly from the mountains, and that along this stream there were large trees and good grass both valuable assets as the winter snows drew near.[20] This river now bears the name of Truckee.

Though the main canyon they had been following turned south, these emigrants determined to strike directly west by the shortest route instead of seeking Walker's Pass to the south. A group of six, however was chosen, to continue the canyon route through Walker's Pass on horseback in order to acquaint Captain Sutter with the needs of the emigrant band moving through the Sierras.[21]

The main body with the wagons went west a few miles until they came to the lake since known as Donner Lake. Here they camped to explore the region in order to manage the wagons.[22] Ultimately, a second division of the Stevens-Murphy party seemed advisable. The owners of six wagons containing some valuable cargo arranged to leave these supplies near Donner Lake until the following spring;[23] three of the younger men volunteered to remain as guards.[24] The other members then set out with the five remaining wagons and all the oxen to scale the Sierras by way of the Truckee River and Pass. The penetration of the mountains made in the fall and early winter was accompanied by great hardship; swollen streams impeded their progress and wagon beds became improvised ferries for men and supplies. The challenge was great, yet it was their decision to head directly west that brought the emigrants safely through as the trail breakers of the Truckee route.[25]

November of 1844 marks the opening of this California trail.[26] The journey down the western slope of the Sierras brought the travelers to the upper waters of the Yuba River.[27] With winter at hand and the birth of a new member of the party expected, another encampment became necessary.[28] The men set about storing the five wagons, butchering cattle, and constructing cabins where the women and children remained during the winter of 1844-45 under the protection of James Miller and the elderly Mr. Martin.[29] The remaining able-bodied men continued the descent of the Sierras' western slope and with no special difficulty arrived a week later at Sutter's fort. The six members of the horseback party had reached the fort a few days before.

It was not until March of 1845 that all the groups of the Stevens-Murphy were reunited. Early in that year, Martin Murphy, Jr., with a party from Sutter's fort, reentered the mountains to rescue the women and children. The winter had been long and hazardous; by March the food supply was almost exhausted.[30] This final phase of the journey west proved the valor of the pioneer women.

The Stevens-Murphy party preceded the Forty-Niners by five years; they also claim two other distinctions. The first wheel tracks from the midwestern states, across the Sierras, and on to the settled portion of California were those of the Stevens-Murphy wagons.[31] Secondly, these immigrants were the first American settlers to reach the crest of the Sierra divide by way of the Truckee River, thus opening the central immigrant trail and discovering a route used later by the first transcontinental railroad.[32]

The journey required wonderful faith and resolution, energy and perseverance. Pioneers of the 1840's in quest of new homes and fortunes were part of the irresistible human current that swept beyond the Sierras to the Pacific and in the forefront of those pathfinders the Martin Murphys stand out.

CHAPTER III

IN THE SACRAMENTO VALLEY

In the 1840's the northern part of California gave promise of agricultuarl development, but, for a time, the Gold Rush channeled the energies of men into easier roads to prosperity.[1] John Augustus Sutter a native of Switzerland, arrived in the Sacramento Valley in 1839. In 1841 he procured a grant of eleven leagues[2] of land from the Mexican Government and built his colony of New Helvetia near the confluence of the Sacramento and American rivers. It is clear from various records that Martin Murphy, Jr. was associated with John A. Sutter in the building of New Helvetia.

Sutter's one great objective was to make money and under whatever flag this was done was of little consequence to him.[3] The welcome and aid which American immigrants received from Sutter, must be credited with a large share in the later direction of public events in California. In the 1840's Sutter's settlement became a haven for the vanguard of emigrants from the United States.[4] They were good customers coming often to Sutter's fort to exchange food and cattle for wagons, seed, and implements. Emigrants found work on Sutter's land as grain fields spread and the herds increased.[5]

Mexican authorities grew suspicious of Sutter's regard for foreigners, whom they themselves were none too anxious to welcome. A statement by Sutter in the preface to the *New Helvetia Diary* tells of his position under Mexican rule in California.

Alvarado hesitated to bestow on me an official military title for fear of General Vallejo's displeasure yet when Micheltorena came into power (1842) he accorded me the military title of captain. At this time, strange to set down, I had full power of life and death over both Indians and white people in my section of Northern California . . . I encouraged American immigration and occupancy of this new land and the Mexicans discouraged it. I sympathized with and respected the Americans who came to this new empire. It was of such men that I planned to build New Helvetia into a sovereign state.[6]

Manuel Micheltorena had been appointed Governor of California by Mexican authorities in 1842. His predecessor, Juan Bautista Alvarado, was determined to resist Micheltorena's authority. When the Stevens-Murphy party arrived in California in December of 1844, a revolution was in progress.[7] There was no sufficient reason for the foreign residents to take part in the quarrel, but apparently many of them chose sides for motives largely based on personal interest.[8] Sutter supported Micheltorena and his efforts to enlist in his ranks the twenty-one newly arrived men of the Stevens-Murphy group were successful.

On January 1, 1845, the "army" of Sutter marched southward to San Jose and along the Salinas River.[9] After a period of service in the campaign, the Murphys and thirty-five others received permission from Micheltorena to return to the Sacramento area.[10] For the Murphys, there was the unfinished business of bringing the women and children down from the winter camp in the Sierras where they had been living since December. Therefore, in March of 1845, a group including Martin Murphy, Jr., that had left Sutter's fort on the American River, conducted the last members of the Stevens-Murphy party down into the Sacramento Valley.

In the summer of 1845, Martin Murphy, Jr. purchased for $250 "Rancho de Ernesto" from Ernest Rufus, a German settler. The property extended for two square leagues on the bank of the Cosumnes River and was about eighteen miles from Sutter's fort. [11]

The Bear Flag Revolt of June, 1846, the first in a series of events which ended with California's becoming part of the United States, was initiated on Murphy's Ranch on the Cosumnes River.[12] Lieutenant Francisco Arce, representing Mexican jurisdiction, had placed horses which he was driving from the Sonoma Valley to the San Jose area in the corral of Martin Murphy's ranch.

The first week of June, Lieutenant Arce, with eleven soldiers in bringing 170 horses and mares belonging to his General, Castro, then at Headquarters, Santa Clara Mission, had to cross the Sacramento near New Helvetia. One morning while eating at their campfires, at the house of Martin Murphy of Ireland, was visited by one Merritt an American, one O'Farlen (Irish) and ten other foreigners, who demanded their guns and horses, which without resistance were given up. Lieutenant Arce and party were then allowed their arms, the horses under the saddle and a fresh horse each . . . the parties then parted, the foreigners carrying off 80 to 100 saddle horses and mares.[13]

When this band of American settlers led by Ezekeil Merritt captured the horses and led them back to the American settlements, they committed themselves to rebellion against the Mexican Government.[14] This incident initiated revolt in the Sacramento Valley and the first act for American control in California had occurred. The Bear Flag Revolt culminated in the short-lived Republic of California which lasted twenty-five days, June 14, to July 9, 1846.

Martin Murphy remained on the Cosumnes Rancho until 1849 raising the first wheat ever grown in the Sacramento Valley.[15] The entries in Sutter's *Diary* refer to Murphy's visits to New Helvetia as well as the wagon loads of wheat brought to the fort from his rancho.[16] Little progress had been made in agriculture prior to 1842. Sutter had bought the improvements at Fort Ross in 1841, but had no wheat with which to make the first payment to the Russians.[17] Settlers residing in the Sacramento area before gold was discovered found raising stock far more profitable than agriculture since land was cheap and pasturage ample. Murphy, despite the contemporary allurement of quick wealth through prospecting, preferred farming. His agricultural success and specialty in wheat farming was an asset to Sutter's growing settlement of New Helvetia.

The foundations for Murphy's future wealth were laid during his residence on this rancho in the Sacramento Valley. The profits from wheat were so large that he was enabled to make other land purchases in New Helvetia.[18] Two lots adjacent to the present site of Sutter's fort were bought from John A. Sutter, Jr., for $500, two others from John A. Sutter, Sr., for $15[19] A portion of another piece of property which Martin Murphy acquired was leased to the California Stage Company for their first terminal in Sacramento established in 1854.[20]

While living in his first California home on the Cosumnes River, Murphy's concern for the education of his children prompted him to start a school reminiscent of Ireland's hedge-schools. Patrick O'Brien entered the Murphy home as tutor; the classes conducted for other children as well as the Murphys constituted the first school established in the Sacramento Valley.

About the first thing he did after taking possession of his new home was to look around for a school teacher. This he found in the person of one Patrick O'Brien, an educated man, who having become reduced in circumstances, had joined the army. He came across the mountains with Fremont and probably deserted. While engaged in teaching at Murphy's, General Sherman, then a lieutenant, arrested him and took him away. We understand however that he was finally released. This was the first school ever held in the Sacramento County.[21]

Just as the home in Canada had been a haven for travelers, so on the remote Cosumnes Rancho the tradition of Murphy hospitality was continued.[22] The "Ranch is often mentioned by travelers between the bay and Sacramento," and several noteworthy persons made brief visits.[23] In the *New Helvetia Diary* Sutter mentions that Captain John C. Fremont stayed at the Murphy Rancho in June of 1847 making it his home base of supply and operations while his soldiers rested and explored the surrounding territory.[24] In the business of selling horses and cattle to Fremont, Murphy had occasion to meet members of his party which included Kit Carson,[25] Alex Godey,[26] and other well-known frontiersmen. General William T. Sherman tells in his *Memoirs* that when traveling from Monterey to Sutter's fort he and his party spent the night with the Murphy family.[27] In 1849, Bayard Taylor made a tour of California as correspondent for the New York *Tribune,* then owned by Horace Greeley. An interesting account of his visit to the Murphy place is given in *Eldorado or Adventures in the Path of Empire:*

About two hours after dark, however, a faint light glimmered in the distance, and I finally reached the place of my destination — Murphy's Rancho on the Cosumnes River. An Indian boy tied my horse to a haystack, and Mrs. Murphy set about making some biscuit in a pan, and roasting a piece of beef for me on a wooden spit. A company of gold-diggers, on their way from the Yuba to winter on the Mariposa, had possession of one end of the house, where they lay rolled in their blankets, their forms barely discernible through the smoke sent out by the rainsoaked wood of which their fire was made. I talked an hour with them about the prospects of mining on the different rivers, and then lay down to sleep on the clay floor . . . Mr. Murphy, I found was the son of the old gentleman whose hospitalities I had shared in the valley of San Jose. He had been living three years on the river, and his three sturdy sons could ride and throw a lariat equal to any Californian.[28]

Martin Murphy represents the pioneer group of settlers of the 1840's by whom the actual occupation of California was effected.[29] They came to establish permanent homes, and to be identified inseparably with the new land; but in 1844, when the Murphys arrived, the old California stood close to the end of its tranquil romantic day. The keynote to the period from 1846 to 1850 was the struggle for civil government. The outdated system of government adjusted to the simple wants of a pastoral people was suddenly called on to serve the needs of a rapidly growing, aggressive population. American settlers recently arrived from the western states resented the military government. Difficulties were not solved even at the end of the Mexican War with the cession of the California area to the United States in 1848.[30] A letter by Senator Thomas Hart Benton appeared in the *Daily Alta* concerning the political situation in California after 1848:

The treaty with Mexico makes you citizens of the United States. Congress has not yet passed the laws to give you the blessings of our government, and it may be some time before it does so. In the meantime while your condition is anomalous and critical, it calls for the most exalted patriotism on your part. The temporary civil and military government established over you as a right of war is at an end . . . Having no lawful government, nor lawful officers, you can have none except by your own act; you can have none that can have authority over you except by your own consent.[31]

The unsettled conditions in California extended to areas other than political. Within a year after the discovery of gold in 1848, activity in the Sacramento area changed from agricultural pursuits to those of mining. The immigrants to the valley in 1849 were for the most part single men and gold seekers in search of a location for prospecting.[32] The lawlessness in the mining camps affected the ranches through cattle rustling, theft, and open plunder. As the population increased, general disregard for citizens' rights took the form of a "squatter" problem for property owners.[33]

As one of the business men and one who constituted the more responsible part of the American population, Martin Murphy observed that the future of the Sacramento area would center in speculative enterprises for some years to come. Conservative in outlook, Murphy had no part in the gold rush or resulting speculation. However, the qualities of an astute business man helped him to utilize to his advantage the existing conditions in the mining section of the state. Large profits accrued when the influx of people into California's gold country brought demand for meat, thus expanding the cattle owners' market. The price of land also increased so that in 1850 Martin Murphy was able to sell half of his rancho on the Cosumnes River, together with 3,000 head of cattle, for $50,000.[34] He reserved 640 acres, including the homestead where the family continued to live while a new location was in preparation.[35]

Many factors contributed to the selection of the fourth and last home site for this pioneer family. Though hospitality was one of the marks of the Murphy home, miners and other transient visitors did not contribute to an atmosphere of order and refinement needed for the young Murphys. Both business trips and visits to his father's home in the San Jose region acquainted Martin, Jr. with the Santa Clara area south of the San Francisco Bay.[36] There, land was available, cattle raising and wheat farming profitable, and finally, as on two former occasions since leaving Ireland, his father's magnetic influence drew him to the family circle. Here,

14

too, the Mission Church in Santa Clara would provide the benefits of religion.

As far as can be determined, Martin Murphy's residence on the Cosumnes River rancho terminated in the early part of 1850. During the next decade his acquisition of large tracts of land in central California southward to San Luis Obispo not only placed him among California's largest landholders but also among the successful business men in the cattle and wheat industries of the state.

CHAPTER IV

THE MURPHY RANCHOS

Americans entering California between 1830 and 1846 were recipients of many land grants. Spain had made generous grants of land to former soldiers, but a greater number of grants can be traced to the period of Mexican rule after 1821.

The Mexican governor was permitted to grant vacant public lands in tracts not larger than eleven square leagues (c. 48,000 acres) to any one applicant. Before a complete title could be vested in a grantee, certain formalities were prescribed: (1) A petition stating citizenship must be presented to the governor by the party asking the grant of land;[1] (2) the citizen must be the head of a family, and in need of grazing lands to maintain flocks and herds, and (3) a description of the tract desired must be presented together with a sketch called a *deseno*.[2]

Murphy came into California in 1844 when Mexican jurisdiction still prevailed. As in Quebec and Missouri, so now in California his need for land was urgent in order to provide for a growing family. Abiding by existing law and wisely making provision for his future needs as a resident in Mexican territory, he petitioned the government for naturalization papers as a citizen of the Mexican Republic on January 28, 1846.[3] His residence in New Helvetia was attested to by John A. Sutter, Sr., and a second witness, Jose Castro, certified that Martin Murphy had lived two years in California and observed good conduct.[4]

There is no record of his having used his privileges as a Mexican citizen in a direct application for or reception of a grant of land from his adopted country. The Murphy papers, however, provide ample evidence of his purchase of land from residents of California, many of whom, if one can judge by names, were Mexican citizens.[5] The first purchase of the Cosumnes River rancho from Ernest Rufus proved successful for wheat farming, but by 1848 the economic conditions in the mining section of the state interfered with specializing in agriculture. Furthermore, climatic conditions near the Sacramento River were similar to those of the Missouri area and Bernard Murphy explains in his Dictation that "We had been troubled with our old enemy chills and fever in the Sacramento Valley and Father thought this [Santa Clara County] would prove a healthier location."[6]

The opportunity to acquire the new homesite in the Santa Clara

Valley, Pastoria de las Borregas,[7] occurred in a singular way. His son, Bernard D., gives the account in the Dictation:

In 1849 my father was trading with the miners, supplying them with cattle and horses, and he came down here intending to purchase a band of cattle to take up to the mines. The owner here would not sell at the agreed price. Father had the money with him, as it was at that time customary to carry large sums of money about the person, and accordingly he bought the rancho Pastoria De Las Voregus [sic] (meaning sheep pasture) . . . My father went to Judge Wallace to get him to draw up the deed for him, he paying five dollars per acre for the land, and Wallace said to him 'Old man, you have the h--l of a lot of nerve to settle in that wild country.' We all moved down bag and baggage.[8]

Partial settlement of the purchase of this rancho was negotiated in 1849, a politically unsettled period following the Mexican War. At this time there was probably not a perfect title to land in the whole territory of Alta California,[9] and this property, as well as other locations acquired by him, came under the scrutiny of the United States Land Commission during the decade of the 1850's.[10] The ranch Pastoria de las Borregas, better known in connection with the Murphy family as "Bay View," had been granted in 1842 by Governor Juan Bautista Alvarado to Francisco Estrada.[11] His heir, Jose Mariano Estrada, ceded it to Mariano Castro,[12] who in 1851 transferred the ownership of the rancho to Martin Murphy in exchange for $12,000.[13] Acreage was added to the original land grant on two occasions. One purchase followed the decision of the United States Land Commission which confirmed a strip of land as the property of Murphy's neighbor, Mariano Castro. Rather than move his fence over, Murphy purchased the land from Castro for $300.[14]

Such undefined limits of land grants from the Spanish-Mexican regimes constituted one of the most serious causes of disputed titles, and of endless boundary litigation that characterized the decade of the fifties. The Land Commission adjudged Martin Murphy's claim to Pastoria de las Borregas in July 1854

. . . that claim of the said petitioner is valid and it is therefore decreed that the same be confirmed. The lands of which confirmation are hereby made, are part of the place known by the name of Pastoria de las Borregas which place is bounded and described as follows: . . .[15]

The ownership of this property remained under court procedure until 1860 at which time Murphy's ownership was final.[16] Ultimately, all of the extensive Murphy Ranchos were verified, surveyed, and listed as "Private Grants" with clearance of title.

Pastoria de las Borregas was a 4,000-acre tract bordering the San Francisco Bay about twelve miles northwest of San Jose where the present city of Sunnyvale is located.[17] The rancho lost its Spanish title in favor of the more familitar one of "Murphy Ranch" or "Bay View Ranch."[18] The house built thereon was not one of the traditional adobe, but the first frame house erected in the Santa Clara County. It "was milled to specifications in Bangor, Maine, shipped around the Horn in prefabricated sections and put together with wooden pegs and rawhide thongs"[19] by a carpenter in San Francisco named Dawson who received 500 acres of land for the work of construction.[20]

In this home, hospitality was offered to all and no one in need was ever turned away from it.[21] The latchstring always hung outside the door and plenty was found within.[22] Until 1961 the historic Murphy house stood on Sunnyvale Avenue between Arques and California Streets in the suburbs of the town.[23] It merited a place in *Historic Spots in California*:

The house was kept in excellent condition having been regularly painted and cared for by a thrifty and intelligent family. It is of two stories, with the stairs leading to the upper floor in the hall that runs through the center of the house from front to back, with doors opening into the garden at both ends. When the house was put in place, the travel up and down the peninsula passed by its bay side; passenger boats plying between Alviso and San Francisco could be seen from the door, and El Camino Real passed between the house and the Bay. With the coming of the railroad the activities of travel changed to the other side of the dwelling — now the main highway. The ample white house stands in attractive grounds in which immense fig trees grown from Mission cuttings still flourish. Within the house are family portraits, done in oil by various artists, of several generations of fine men and gracious women. To this house walked the priests of Santa Clara Mission to celebrate Mass at regular intervals. A room with an altar and a consecrated altar stone was set apart for the purpose, and here marriage and christening ceremonies took place as well. Mary Bolger kept one of the rooms in the house always ready for the comfort of the Bishop should he stop for a night's rest on his way between the Missions.[24]

Members of the Murphy family occupied this house continuously until 1953. After protracted debates between citizens of Sunnyvale and the City Council[25] regarding the future of this homestead, its destruction was ordered in 1961 and the house ceased to be a segment of Sunnyvale's history except for the landmark plaque which had been erected the previous year, on May 22, 1960.[26]

Several additional extensive holdings established Murphy's reputation as "the largest individual land owner and cattle raiser on the central coast."[27] In Santa Barbara County, Point Concepcion

Rancho stretched over 12,000 acres;[28] La Purissima Concepcion in Santa Clara County, 5,000 acres;[29] Milpitas Rancho in Santa Clara County held only 800 acres, but was one of the tracts which showed increasing value in the years after 1866.[30]

Martin Murphy exercised an acute judgement in his selection of property; he possessed an almost prophetic view regarding the areas of California's future economic growth. By the time the railroad builders brought development to the central part of California, Murphy had become the owner of thousands of acres.[31] He acquired in the 1860's three adjoining Mexican ranchos in the San Luis Obispo County: Santa Margarita, Atascadero, and Asuncion along the Salinas River.[32] Documents among the Murphy papers reveal the varying circumstances which accompanied the change of ownership for these three ranchos.

Santa Margarita was a land grant to Joaquin Estrada by Governor Manuel Jimeño in 1841.[33] Financial problems caused Senor Estrada to borrow money; for security he used his Rancho Santa Margarita, a tract of over 17,000 acres.[34] In the Murphy Papers is a promissary note for $20,000 entered into by Joaquin Estrada and a partnership including Martin Murphy of Santa Clara County and Peter Donahue of the City and County of San Francisco.[35] During the course of 1860, Senor Estrada went deeper into debt to Murphy by mortgaging both his Santa Margarita and Atascadero ranchos for $5,000.[36]

To financial distress suffered by the Estrada family was added the uncertainty of title and boundaries of this heavily mortgaged domain. As in the case of other California Land grants, the survey and verification of ownership of Santa Margarita Rancho was in process. Confirmation of title was issued to Joaquin Estrada in 1861;[37] and, after this clearance of title, Murphy negotiated the purchase of Santa Margarita. The Indenture among the Murphy Papers indicates that Murphy paid Joaquin Estrada $45,000.[38] It is to be noted that Santa Margarita was purchased and did not pass into the ownership of Murphy by foreclosure; the case is in support of the traditional reputation that Martin Murphy had of never foreclosing a mortgage.[39]

Atascadero, another of the San Luis Obispo ranchos, extended over 4,000 acres. Granted originally by the Mexican Governor Juan Bautista Alvarado to Trifon Garcia, the land subsequently passed to four owners before the last of these, Edward McShane, sold the rancho to Joaquin Estrada.[40] Again, financial need resultant from lavish living forced Senor Estrada to mortgage the land to two merchants of San Luis Obispo County, Nathan Goldtree and Morris Cohen, for $4,750.[41] When Estrada was unable to meet his obligations, Goldtree and Cohen foreclosed the mortgage in August of 1864.[42] Two months thereafter, possibly allowing time for redemption of the property, Goldtree and Cohen sold the Atascadero Rancho to Murphy for $4,750.[43]

The largest of the three ranchos, Asuncion, was an extensive estate of 39,000 acres. The original grant had been made in 1844 by Pio Pico, then Governor of California. In 1864 William Farrell was the owner and from him Martin Murphy purchased this vast estate for $1,000.[44]

For assessment purposes, California ranchos were divided into four classes according to the quality of the soil and the accessibility of their location.[45] Rancho Santa Margarita was judged first class, Rancho Atascadero, second, and Rancho Asuncion, fourth class.[46] As late as the 1880's thousands of head of cattle were pastured on these ranchos and became a source of great wealth.[47] The management of this estate was entrusted to Martin Murphy's son, Patrick W. Murphy, who made the Santa Margarita Rancho his home and business headquarters.[48]

Murphy Home in the Santa Clara Valley.

CHAPTER V

CITIZEN OF SAN JOSE

The desire for religious and educational advantages had been a controlling factor in the careers of the Martin Murphys.[1] Religious sentiments had induced them to cross the plains to California in 1844. An opportunity to realize the educational objective came to Martin Murphy shortly after his arrival in the Santa Clara Valley. This project became the first in a series of notable philanthropies.

Bishop Joseph Sadoc Alemany became the Bishop of the Californias in the same year that the Murphys began residence on the Pastoria de las Borregas Rancho. When the Bishop arrived in San Francisco in 1850,[2] he assumed the task of caring for a Catholic community of 40,000 in a total population of 150,000 in the state of California. There were twenty-eight priests in charge of twenty-six churches and a seminary. From his headquarters in Monterey he was obliged to journey far, making visitations of parishes, conferring confirmation, and blessing new churches and schools in his vast diocese.[3] The Murphy home was often the stopping place for the Bishop on his journey south; a room was designated as the "Bishop's room" and there he celebrated Mass.[4] The friendship of Martin Murphy with Bishop Alemany was strong and fruitful for the growth of Catholicism in California since "the old gentleman used to contribute to Bishop Allemany [sic] for churches in every direction."[5]

The new Bishop set about rebuilding the Santa Clara Mission, then in a state of disrepair resulting from secularization, and he reorganized the Church by appointing priests to parishes. Bernard Murphy relates interesting facts about his father's help to Bishop Alemany who was eager to bring the influence of the Church back to the Santa Clara Valley:

About 1850 Bishop Allemany [sic] arrived. Up to that time the churches had been abandoned. He reorganized the Catholic Church here, as it then stood, repaired the mission buildings, and put in new priests. In this work he was largely aided in a financial way by my father. The ranche [sic] was always his headquarters whenever he visited this section, and it was father who suggested to him to start a school in Santa Clara.[6]

The establishment of the College of Santa Clara was one of the achievements sponsored by Bishop Alemany in which Martin

Murphy played a vital part. In 1849 Father Gonzales Rubio, O.F.M. administrator of the Monterey Diocese, made an urgent request for priests to care for the Catholic immigrants. A group of Jesuits were sent from Oregon to California and among them was Father Joseph Nobili who was stationed at Santa Clara.[7] In 1851, on Murphy suggestion, Bishop Alemany appointed Father Nobili as the first president of the College of Santa Clara.[8] His further patronage and liberality gave Murphy a right to share the honors of founding that institution.[9]

Martin Murphy had great regard for learning and the events of his life gave credence to the statement that "Irish who have emigrated to the American continent have given touching proof of their devotion to learning."[10] In addition to his interest in Santa Clara College, he gave financial help in 1851 in establishing an academy for girls taught by the Sisters of Notre Dame de Namur in San Jose.

The Sisters of Notre Dame had opened a school in the Willamette Valley in Oregon in 1844. In May of 1851, two Sisters from this group, Sister Loyola Duquenne and Sister Marie Catherine Cabareaux, traveled to San Francisco to meet the ship bringing new members for their community.[11] Life was not without difficulties for the missionaries in Oregon and Father Anthony Langlois, the Vicar forane, who knew of the Sisters' problems, suggested to Bishop Alemany that he persuade Sister Loyola, the Superior, to keep the Sisters in California.[12] As a consequence, the Bishop offered the Sisters a foundation at San Jose, then the State Capital.[13]

During the two months of waiting for the vessel to arrive from Panama the Sisters accepted Murphy's invitation to visit his family at Bay View.[14] They accompanied him there on April 2, 1851, and during their stay the Sisters "met kind friends and heard earnest solicitations and pressing invitations" to make the valley a place of their teaching. Many of those who urged them to stay were early pioneers who had experienced the lack of educational advantages and were eager to help the Sisters in establishing a school.[15]

While at Bay View the Sisters had an opportunity to visit San Jose and Santa Clara where they met Father Joseph Nobili, S.J. in the midst of formative plans for Santa Clara College. As a result of these visits the Sisters were encouraged to open a school. The time seemed opportune since offers of land and financial assistance cleared away some of the difficulties.[16] In August 1851 the Sisters of Notre Dame opened their academy in San Jose in a small building which was soon supplemented with a larger one to meet the needs of over one hundred boarders.[17] This establishment later developed into the College of Notre Dame which in 1924 moved to the Ralston estate in Belmont, California.

Martin Murphy's participation in the founding of these two institutions of learning[18] was one of his far-reaching philanthropies, but activities in other fields of interest have also made him memorable. As the largest individual landowner on the central coast,[19] Murphy became recognized as a leader in agriculture and cattle raising in the Santa Clara and San Luis Obispo counties.[20]

From the time Martin Murphy settled in San Jose until the 1860's the people in Sacramento referred to Santa Clara County as "cow country," the source of their supplies of beef. During the next decade property around San Jose increased in value[21] and a consequent shift of the cattle ranches further south took place[22] while orchards, vineyards, and grain crops took priority in the central region of California.[23] Here as he had done in Sacramento, Murphy specialized in wheat farming[24] and his industry in agriculture helped to establish the supremacy of the vast wheat ranches of the Santa Clara Valley. By the 1870's the chief article of produce in the Santa Clara Valley was the superior type of wheat which could bear transportation by sea or land, and storage for an indefinite period of time without damage.[25] In addition to reaping a rich harvest, he prudently safeguarded his produce by insurance against loss by fire. The Commercial Union Assurance Company of London, which had offices in San Francisco, insured tons of wheat stored in the private warehouses at Murphy Station.[26] The high prices for both grain and stock which prevailed insured a handsome revenue.[27]

Murphy's astute business ability combined precision, honesty, and prudent management in avoiding all risks and considering all aspects of a bargain.[28] By the 1860's he had become a citizen of wealth, prominent as a property holder in the business district of San Jose.[29] Where adobe prevailed as the building material, his use of brick was an innovation.[30] One building site in particular became historic; for, at the same time he constructed a brick block of stores on the east side of Market Street,[31] the lease expired for the offices held by city officials. With characteristic civic-mindedness, Murphy offered to finish the upper portion of these new buildings in a manner suitable for government offices. The city officials accepted the proposal and drew up a five-year lease arranging for temporary quarters for the City Hall.[32]

The cares incidental to the management of a large estate did not hinder Murphy from participation in the civic life of California. Citizenship gained by being a resident of California when it became a state was later verified by his certificate of citizenship.[33] He voted for the first time in 1850[34] and registered as "Irish" and as "Farmer" in the Mountin View Electoral District in the 1860's and 1870's.[35] The Society of California Pioneers[36] honored him with membership in that exclusive group in 1853.[37]

Though not inclined to seek a position of political leadership for himself, Murphy's interest and influence helped to direct California's policy. His political affiliations were within the Democratic party; during the Civil War the family remained Democratic though they were classed as Union Democrats. On the issue of slavery Murphy was conservative. Strongly in favor of the Union, he stood for Lincoln's proposal for compensated emancipation of the slaves.[38] The San Jose *Weekly Patriot,* which was started in 1863, became Democratic in the 1870's under ownership of the Murphys and changed its title to San Jose *Daily Herald.[39]* Bernard attests to his father's interest in politics:

Father was always an active member of the Democratic Party. He never sought for any office and would not have one if he could get it, but he always had his shoulder to the wheel of his party.[40]

Bernard considered that his democratic ideas extended to the family: "He was always democratic in his tendencies, in fact the whole Murphy family is democratic and has been so, from the beginning as far as is known."[41]

As a progressive citizen, Murphy interested himself in the development of transportation within the state of California. In 1863, the same year that tracks were laid through the Sierras by the Central Pacific Railroad[42] along the route opened by the Stevens-Murphy party, a local line began operations between San Francisco and San Jose using a "right of way" grant through Pastoria de las Borregas.[43] A new business center gradually sprang up around the depot at Murphy's ranch, henceforth known as Murphy's Station. In a rapidly developing agricultural area, depots were needed to facilitate the transportation of grain by the railroads.[44] Murphy funds for local improvements included the building of Lawrence Station halfway between Sunnyvale and Santa Clara.[45]

Murphy showed his charitable attitude in his dealings with "squatters;" his regard for them is "peculiarly noteworthy as an almost solitary example of its kind."[46] Many American immigrants

24

came to California from states where public land was abundant, hence they were inclined to view large ranchos as public domain. When squatters settled on land of the Pastoria de las Borregas Rancho, Murphy condoned their trespass on his property with charity while Mrs. Murphy ministered to their needs for food and clothing.[47] The "squatters" consequently withdrew without the bitterness which often resulted from such encounters.

Another aspect of Murphy's character may be noted through the use he made of his fortune to help others. Though wary of his own business ventures, evidence can be found in the Murphy Papers of his willingness to stand bond for others' debts.[48] Numerous promissary notes, frequently written on scraps of paper, reveal his generous loans to people in various stations of life and at low rates of interest.[49] Instances can be cited also of his donations of money or material goods to those in need; the produce of his farm was not only sold but also given away.[50] In lending money Murphy charged a low rate of interest; his gifts never had the character of a dole. His theory in sharing his wealth was "that a man should make his own way, but he would help him to chances to make it."[51]

The traditional generosity and hospitality of the Murphy household reached an unprecedented level on the occasion of the Murphy's Golden Wedding Anniversary, July 18, 1881. The Murphy Ranch was the scene of the "most fabulous social event ever held in California."[52] Rather than risk oversights when sending announcements, the elderly couple extended a general invitation to their many friends throughout the state by a notice in the San Jose *Daily Mercury*.[53] The hundreds of guests who visited them that day demonstrated the high esteem which the people of California held for Martin and Mary Murphy.[54] Those unable to attend sent congratulatory letters to the Jubilarians commenting on their noble lives, their deeds of kindness, and their honored place among the builders of California.[55]

Soon after this gala event Martin Murphy's health began to fail. Until his seventy-fourth year he was a man of exceptionally good physique. In 1880 while on a business trip to San Francisco, he fell and broke his leg. Though the injury was not great, the shock was so severe that his health was affected.[56] He continued to live at the Murphy Rancho until 1882 when by medical advice he moved to a residence in San Jose. In 1883 he suffered a heart attack from which he never fully recovered. Realizing the danger of death at any moment, Martin and his wife divided their property equally among their heirs and made joint deeds of trust for the holding of their property until Martin's death.[57] True business man to the end, he had set all his affairs in order. The following year Martin Murphy died on October 20, 1884. "Santa Clara's most respected, most popular, and oldest citizen."[58]

The San Francisco *Morning Call* gave notice of the event under the title "Death of a Well-Known Pioneer and Millionaire:"

Martin Murphy foremost of pioneers and widely known for his wealth and generous hospitality died of heart disease about 3 o'clock yesterday morning (Oct. 20) at his residence in San Jose. The life of Martin Murphy is worthy of study in these days of shifting occupations and gambling speculations.[59]

Deeper sentiments were expressed in the San Jose *Mercury* account:

Seldom has an event transpired within the city's history that has caused so general a feeling of sadness and regret as the death of Martin Murphy. This was testified to by the large number of people who visited the home of the bereaved family. Many were comparative strangers who, actuated by a knowledge of the good deeds of Martin Murphy, desired to look for the last time on a face they had learned to love.[60]

The obsequies were held at St. Joseph Church in San Jose in the presence of a large congregation of family and friends. Archbishop Alemany celebrated a solemn Requiem Mass and gave the final blessing to Martin Murphy. In an eloquent oration, Father John Prendergast of St. Mary Cathedral in San Francisco reviewed "the life and extolled the many admirable traits of character of the deceased."[61] The day was one of mourning for the community of San Jose; flags were at half mast, the City Hall and business houses were closed.[62] On the way to the cemetery in Santa Clara where another large group of friends awaited, the cortege of two hundred vehicles passed the Convent of Notre Dame where an honor guard of Sisters and students paid their last tribute to the friend and patron of the Academy.[63]

The mantle of Martin Murphy, Sr. had descended on his eldest son Martin, and all the traits which characterized the founder of the family were developed in him in a greater degree: "Strict but not over-harsh in business matters, liberal but unobtrusive in charities, warm as a friend, generous as a foe, and prompt in all things, were the well-known characteristics of Martin Murphy, Jr."[64]

CONCLUSION

The forces stirred by economic unrest in the early nineteenth century caused a chain of events that brought Martin Murphy, Jr. from Ireland to California in 1844. His life encompasses the early immigration period of the United States, turbulence of the Gold Rush days in the Sacramento Valley, and the confused land grant period of the 1850's in the San Jose region.

Ireland saw some of her promising sons leave for the New World. California attracted adventurous individuals even before the cry of "Gold." One group of far-seeing individuals came to wrest from the land an adequate living denied them in Ireland. The two-thousand-mile trek from Missouri to California consequently was undertaken by valiant immigrants who for the first time brought wagons from Missouri over the California Trail as early as 1844.

California, still under the control of Mexico, was being exploited by local officials particularly in regard to the secularized mission lands. Martin Murphy early recognized the potential agricultural resources of the territory and secured a land grant, first in the Sacramento Valley and later replaced it by one in the Santa Clara area. Within six years, as a result of the Gold Rush and the Mexican War, California, now a part of the United States, became a sparsely-settled land of mining camps and urban settlements in the north, but cattle ranchos dominated the southern half.

After achieving statehood in 1850, California continued attracting gold-seekers, yet some pioneers engaged in the political life of the new state, and other self-reliant men who did not aspire to political leadership entered business. By their energy and influence these men contributed in large measure to the shaping of California's political institutions and to developing the economic prosperity of their locality.

Martin Murphy stands out as an example of an acute business man who acquired the extensive grant of Pastoria de las Borregas Rancho, now the site of Sunnyvale, where he first raised cattle and later grew wheat. He used his ranch profits to make loans at low rates to other settlers who needed a start in life and he became one of the influential builders of San Jose. Though a man of little book-learning himself, he showed interest in education by his generous support of Santa Clara College and Notre Dame Academy. He manifested outstanding loyalty to the Catholic Church both in his personal life and in his help to Archbishop Joseph Alemany who was struggling to build up the Archdiocese of San Francisco. At the time of his death in 1884, Martin Murphy held an honored place in the local and regional community. He left a numerous family to carry on the stalwart principles that he had shown in the integrity of his character.

Richard Henry Dana in his *Two Years Before the Mast* commented on the inefficiency of people in the period of the 1830's when California was under Mexican government: "In the hands of an enterprising people what a country this might be." Martin Murphy illustrated by his career what an enterprising man could achieve in his life-span as a citizen of California after it became a part of the United States.

FOOTNOTES

NOTES ON CHAPTER I

1   Ballynamought (**baile** or **bally** means town) means town of the poor people. P. W. Joyce, **The Origin and History of Irish Names and Places** (New York: Logmans, Green and Company, 1901), p. 16.

The embellished account which Bancroft gives in the **Chronicles** regarding the origin of the Murphy family lacks source references and is only to attract the general reader. During a visit to Ireland in May, 1967, the writer visited Wexford and sought unsuccessfully to locate Martin Murphy's birthplace, Balnamough.

2   Murphy Family Chronology found among the Murphy Papers and dated May 31, 1943 (Appendix 3).

3   James, born in 1809; Margaret, 1811; Joanna, 1813; Mary, 1816; Bernard, 1818. **Ibid.**

4   Anthony Marmion, **The Ancient and Modern History of the Maritime Ports of Ireland** (London: W. H. Cox, 1858), pp. 579-580. Modern Wexford is a thriving industrial town and progress has not spelled destruction for memorials of the city's historic past. Reminiscent of its past success in wheat farming, Wexford today is world renowned for for its agricultural machinery. Culturally, the name Wexford has become synonymous with first-class music and opera and the annual Wexford Festival represents high standards of performance. **Official Guide to Wexford,** Wexford Chamber of Commerce, pp. 13-15.

5   E. E. Evans, **Irish Heritage** (Dundalk, W. Tempest: Dundalgan Press, 1949), p. 86. To a large extent Wexford was populated with former immigrants from Western England and Brabant. The section was one of the least Gaelic counties in the Island. Roger Chauvire, **A Short History of Ireland** (New York: The Devin-Adair Co., 1956), p. 105.

6   The Dublin Society of United Irishmen was founded on November 9, 1971. Its manifesto stated: "We have no national government. We are ruled by Englishmen and the servants of Englishmen," and went on to call for "an equal representation of all people in Parliament." James O'Connor, **History of Ireland 1798-1924** (London: Edward Arnold and Co., 1925), p. 64.

7   O'Connor, **op cit.**, p. 193. "Both the Bulgers [sic] and the Murphys were mixed up in the rebellion of 1798, which was one of the things that made the country too warm for them." Murphy Dictation, p. 3 (cf. Preface, p. iii). Alfred Bates MS of Bernard D. Murphy's Dictation is in the Bancroft Library, University of California, Berkeley.

8   O'Connor, **op. cit.**, p. 282.

9   Evans, **op. cit.**, p. 36. Evan today, Wexford's claim is "The Sunny South East." **Official Guide to Wexford,** p. 10.

10   O'Connor, **op. cit.**, pp. 191 f.

11   Lecky, **History of Ireland,** I, 233.

12   **Ibid.,** p. 148.

13 These hedge-schools were conducted in illegal secrecy by wandering masters not always the most respectable type. Chauvire, **op. cit.**, p. 78. "The hedge-school in its most elemental state was an open-air daily assemblage of youths in pursuit of knowledge. The hedge-school master conducted the rites." Joseph Dunn, **The Glories of Ireland** (Washington, D.C.: Phoenix Limited, 1914), p. 40.

14 Lecky, **op. cit.**, III, 350.

15 O'Connor, **op. cit.**, p. 217.

16 Thirty-one years after the Union, Parliament took up efficiently and on a large scale the task of education of the Irish people. Lecky, **op. cit.**, V, 425-426.

17 Documents among the Murphy Papers show the name of Martin Murphy accompanied with +, "his mark" (Appendix 6).

18 "His boys were the first to enter the Santa Clara College at Santa Clara Cal, and by his patronage and liberality he became in a large measure the founder of that great institution. . . . His daughters were likewise the first to enter Notre Dame College at San Jose Cal, and by his patronage and liberality he became in a large measure the founder of that great institution." Letter of William R. McQuoid to H. H. Bancroft, Sept. 13, 1888. MS in Bancroft Library, University of California, Berkeley.

19 Lecky, **op. cit.**, I, 157.

20 "Martin Murphy, Sr., was a devoted Catholic and my father followed in his footsteps in that direction." Murphy Dictation, p. 2. "The Murphys left Missouri, for the principal reason, that the religious and educational advantages were not of a pleasing character, and came to California because it was a Catholic country — Martin Murphy Jun [sic] was much devoted to his church and religious duty, contributing largely to the support of the Catholic Church." McQuoid, **loc. cit.**

21 H. H. Bancroft, **Chronicles of the Builders of the Commonwealth** (San Francisco: The History Co., 1891), p. 16. The children who accompanied their parents were: James, Joanna, Mary, and Bernard. Martin, aged 13, and Margaret, 9, remained in Ireland until 1828.
    When compiling the **Chronicles,** Bancroft engaged in subscription publishing. The average amount charged per page was $100; a steel engraved portrait was included for the $1,000 contributors. The total subvention for the **Chronicles** amounted to $219,225. J. W. Caughey, **Hubert Howe Bancroft** (Berkeley: University of California Press, 1946), pp. 314-322, **passim.** Bernard D. Murphy paid $3,500 for the account which Bancroft makes of Martin Murphy, Jr. in the **Chronicles.** Harry Harry B. Hambly, "List of Subscribers to **Chronicles of the Builders of the Commonwealth,'** Stating Amount Subscribed and Paid," October, 1936. MS in Bancroft Library, University of California, Berkeley.

22 Bancroft, **Chronicles,** p. 16.

23 No reason has been found for Martin's and Margaret's remaining in Ireland. One fact may be a possible clue: Martin, Jr., who was the oldest son, reached the age of twenty-one in 1828. His father had held a lease-hold on their land, but no landlord was permitted to sell without the consent of the eldest son after he had reached his majority. W. F. Adams, **Ireland and Irish Emigration to the New World from 1815 to**

the **Famin** (New Haven: Yale University Press, 1932), p. 9. It is probable that the sale of the land was negotiated in 1828 by Martin and he and his sister were then free to join their parents in Canada.

24 Bancroft, **Chronicles,** pp. 16-17. Atlantic crossings in the 1820's involved hardship and danger. Sailing vessels were the common type of ship and the trip lasted from one to three months. The fare to Quebec in the 1820's was about thirty shillings (between $3 and $4) and seldom a charge for children. M. A. Jones, **American Immigration** (Chicago: University of Chicago Press, 1960), p. 105.

25 Munro-Fraser, **History of Santa Clara County** (San Francisco: Alley and Bowen, 1881), p. 791.

26 "Father had been married in Quebec to Miss Mary Bulger [sic] also from Wexford. Her people were farmers there." Murphy Dictation, p. 3. In a visit to Wexford in June of 1967, the writer located the Bolger homestead in Oylegate, north of the city of Wexford.

27 "Prior to the erection of a church, Martin Murphy, Sr., invited priests to visit the settlement to celebrate Mass, administer the Sacraments, and instruct the children." "Irish Pioneers of California," **The Monitor,** San Francisco, August 24, 1901.

28 James, born in 1832; Martin J., 1836; Patrick W., 1838; Bernard D., 1841. Murphy Family Chronology (Appendix 3).

29 Brebner, **op. cit.,** p. 209.

30 McInnis, **op. cit.,** p. 201.

31 Brebner, **op. cit.,** p. 220.

32 Bancroft, **op. cit.,** pp. 17 f. There is no account of his journey from Quebec to Missouri, but he arrived at this frontier post just when the interest in migrating to the Pacific Coast was beginning. The Murphys were soon followed to Missouri by many of their former neighbors in Canada. A settlement was formed and named "Irish Grove."

33 "It is interesting to note that in Frampton [Quebec] the Irish had first choice of the land. Having had experience with the bogs of Ireland, they chose the more rolling, higher ground, and the French took the 'bottom land.' To their vast disappointment it was found, that unlike Ireland, the higher ground was rocky and poor like New England, whereas the 'bottom land' was rich and productive. This and the scourge of cholera caused Martin Jr. to follow his father to Missouri." Letter from Mrs. Frank R. Stockton, great granddaughter of Martin Murphy, Jr., June 5, 1968.

34 Bancroft, **Chronicles,** p. 16.

35 Munro-Fraser, **op. cit.,** p. 792.

36 Bancroft, **Chronicles,** p. 18.

37 Platte Purchase: the northwest boundary of Missouri was extended to the Missouri River as a result of the purchase of two million acres from the Indians by the Federal Government in 1836. The price was $7,500 cash together with specified quantities of merchandise. **Dictionary of American History** (New York: Charles Scribner's Sons, 1946), Vol. IV, p. 286.

38 At this time the city of St. Joseph claimed only a few scattered farms and a solitary grist-mill. One well-known figure lived there, Joseph Rubidoux, an old trapper and one of the chief informants on the "paradise of California." R. G. Cleland, **A History of California: The American Period** (New York: The Macmillan Co., 1922), pp. 99 f.

39 Holt was one of the six counties designated in the Platte Purchase.

40 Bancroft, **Chronicles,** p. 18.

41 Bancroft, **Chronicles,** p. 19, and Murphy Family Chronology (Appendix 3).

42 In **Chronicles of the Builders of the Commonwealth,** Bancroft mentions a Father Hookins. In a biography of Father De Smet there are several references to two Fathers Hoecken, S.J. Father Christian Hoecken worked among the Kickapoo Indians of Northern Kansas. Father Adrian Hoecken belonged to the Oregon Mission. E. Laveille, **The Life of Father De Smet** (New York: P. J. Kenedy and Sons, 1915), pp. 78-79 and 95.

"Christian Hoecken had been ordained in Holland as a Diocesan Priest entered the Society in Missouri in 1832 and subsequently worked among the Indians in the mid-west, Nebraska, Kansas, etc. In June 1851 he accompanied Father De Smet to the Upper Missouri and died from Asiatic cholera aboard the river boat St. Ange, June 19, 1851. So far as I know, this was as far West as he ever got." Information drawn from archival material at Gonzaga University, Spokane, Washington, by Father William Schoanberg, S.J. and stated in a letter to the author, March 16, 1964. It was probably Father Christian Hoecken who befriended the Murphys since he worked in the vicinity of Council Bluffs. As far as can be determined, Father Christian Hoecken had never been to California.

43 "A Catholic priest Father Hookens [sic] was with them for some time on his trip through Missouri and told the family much of California saying that it was strictly a Catholic country, in addition to its many natural advantages and this it was that caused them to come here." Murphy Dictation, p. 1.

NOTES ON CHAPTER II

1 H. M. Chittenden, **The American Fur Trade of the Far West** (Stanford: Academic Reprints, 1954), Vol. I, p. 2.

2 Statistics quoted on February 15, 1847 placed the annual value of the St. Louis fur trade for the past forty years between two and three hundred thousand dollars. Ibid., p. 8.

3 One of the counties of the Platte Purchase.

4 Cleland, **op. cit.,** p. 99. John Bidwell was one who pledged to be ready to start west on May, 9, 1841. About fifty people assembled at Sapling Grove and formed the Bartleson-Bidwell Party of 1841, the first band of emigrants to start for California. G. R. Stewart, **The California Trail** (New York: McGraw-Hill Book Co., 1962), pp. 7-8.

5 "Most of the party were pretty well fixed for that time none of them being worth over $2,000." Murphy Dictation p. 2. Quigley states that Irishmen came to California at their own expense without aid from immigration or any societies. Hugh Quigley, **The Irish in California and on the Pacific Coast** (San Francisco: A. Roman and Co., 1878), p. 151.

6 "The Missouri property was sold to neighbors and to settlers who were coming in." Murphy Dictation, p. 9.

7 The Stevens-Murphy party had eleven wagons which in the 1840's cost $120 each. Diary of James Abbey quoted in R. G. Cleland, **A History of California** (New York: The Macmillan Co., 1939), p. 239. They were light-weight wagons, sufficiently strong to carry 2,500 pounds, and were drawn by three or four yoke of oxen or six mules. From Independence, Missouri to Sacramento was a distance of 1,975 miles. This was nearly a five-month journey with ox teams averaging fifteen miles per day. John Frost, **History of the State of California** (New York: Hurst & Co., 1859), p. 203.

8 The numerical strength of the Murphy clan might well have led to trouble, but apparently did not. The Murphys were intelligent and able, and probably realized that cooperation was essential to survival. G. R. Stewart, **The Opening of the California Trail** (Berkeley: University of California, 1953), p. 16.

9 "Grandfather was considered boss of the party and my father next as he was the oldest of four brothers." Murphy Dictation, p. 2.

10 Bancroft states that the second emigrant party of 1844 came under the leadership of Elisha Stevens, though it has been called the Murphy company from the name of a large family, afterward prominent citizens of Santa Clara County which came with it. H. H. Bancroft, **History of California** (San Francisco: The History Co., 1891), Vol. IV, p. 445.

11 From an American point of view the Stevens-Murphy party must be classed as foreign. Nearly all of its members had been born in Ireland or Canada. Stewart, **op. cit.,** p. 15. Members of the party: Family of Martin Murphy, Sr. — Margaret and Ellen; John, Daniel, and Bernard; James and Ann Martin Murphy with daughter Mary; James Miller and Mary Murphy Miller with son William and three unnamed daughters. Family of Martin Murphy Jr. — Wife Mary Bolger Murphy with four sons, James, Martin J., Patrick W., and Bernard D. Dr. and Mrs. Townsend; Allen Montgomery and wife; Moses Schallenberger; Mr. Hitchcock and daughter Mrs. Isabella Patterson with five children —

Isaac, Tedra, Margaret, Helen, and Mary; John Sullivan with sister Mary and two younger brothers, Michael and Robert; Mr. P. Martin and sons Patrick and Dennis; Matthew Harbin; Vincent Calvin; John Flombeau; Oliver Magnent; Joseph E. Foster; Francis Delanet; Edmund Bray; Caleb Greenwood (Old Greenwood) and sons John and Britton; Captain Elisha Stevens. **Ibid.,** pp. 14-15. See also P. T. Conmy, "Stevens-Murphy Party of 1844," mimeographed copy in Bancroft Library, University of California, Berkeley.

12 E. Bray, "Memoirs of a Trip to California," MS in Bancroft Collection, University of California, Berkeley.

13 "The children of Martin Murphy, Sr. seemed to be men and women of strong common sense, and my opinion is that common sense is about as rare as genius. They seemed to be entirely devoid of peculiarities and took a practical reasonable view of everything." Murphy Dictation, p. 2.
The leader of the party, Elisha Stevens, was a blacksmith; Allen Montgomery, a gunsmith; Dr. Townsend, a physician. Those having western experience were Elisha Stevens, John Hitchcock, and Caleb Greenwood. At least twenty of the men were at the height of their physical powers; the women ranged in age from twenty to thirty-six. Stewart, **California Trail,** p. 63.

14 "We met Indian tribes all the time but took them into camp and gave them a lot of game and fresh meat and sometimes we gave them a little bacon or an old blanket . . . One morning in gathering up the outfit and packing the wagons a halter was missing and he accused a chief of the Winnamucka tribe of stealing it. Words followed and Schallenberger rushed to his wagon, seized his gun and was going to shoot when my father rushed in threw up the gun and took it away from him." Murphy Dictation, p. 2.

15 According to Edmund Gray's "Memoirs" the party reached Fort Hall about September 13, 1844.

16 "We traveled as far as Fort Hall in company with another party whose names I have forgotten who left us there and went to Oregon." Murphy Dictation, p. 2.

17 Cleland, **op. cit.,** p. 115.

18 "We had all the provisions we wanted during the trip as the young men kept us supplied with fresh meat and we did not have to touch our stock until the latter part of the journey when game became scarce." Murphy Dictation, p. 2.
The record of the Stevens-Murphy party during their march from Fort Hall to the sink of the Humboldt River is so short as to approach nothing at all. The longest account reads: "The journey down the Humboldt was very monotonous. Each day's events were substantially a repetition of the day before." Stewart, **California Trail,** p. 64. Bray's "Memoirs" state that the party reached the Humboldt Sink on October 24, 1844.

19 Truckee River and Pass were so named in recognition of the help given them by this Paiute Indian. According to Mrs. Sarah Winnamucka Hopkins, granddaughter of Truckee, this was not his name: "Truckee' is an Indian word. It means 'all right' or 'very well'." He apparently used this expression so frequently that the emigrants took it to be his name.

Cecilia M. Murphy, "The Stevens-Murphy Overland Party of 1844" (unpublished Master's thesis, University of California, 1941), n. 28.

20 Bancroft, **Chronicles,** p. 27.

21 John, Daniel, and Ellen Murphy, Mrs. Townsend, Francis Delanet, and Oliver Magnent. This party was the first group of American emigrants to arrive at Lake Tahoe and the first of the Stevens-Murphy party to reach Sutter's fort.

22 This camp became the base of operations for getting the wagons up the granite slopes of the Sierras; superhuman effort was needed to bring the wagons over the mountainous crags. The cabins built by the Murphys were used by the Donner party in 1846. Stewart, **The California Trail,** p. 72.

23 Dr. Townsend had brought some broadcloth, satins, and silks in one of the wagons. The first wagons brought into California came across the plains in 1844 with the Townsend or Stevens party. They were left in the mountains and lay buried under the snow till the following spring, when Moses Schallenberger, Elisha Stevens, who was captain of the party, and others went up and brought some of the wagons down into the Sacramento Valley. No other wagons had ever before reached California across the plains. Milo Quaife, ed., **Echoes of the Past About California,** by General John Bidwell (Chicago: The Lakeside Press, 1928), p. 86.

24 Joseph Foster, Allen Montgomery, and Moses Schallenberger. Hard times came upon this group during the winter. A week of heavy snowfall at Donner Lake made hunting and gathering firewood impossible. Facing starvation, Foster and Montgomery succeeded in joining the larger group again. Moses Schallenberger, too ill to travel, stayed at Donner Lake until he was rescued by Dennis Martin in February, 1845. **Ibid.** For the full text of Moses Schallenberger's narrative, see Stewart, **The Opening of the California Trail,** pp. 46-84.

25 To appreciate the courage of this attempt it must be remembered that these emigrants were from the flat lands of the Middle West and had had no experience with alpine conditions. "Obviously the leaders of the Stevens-Murphy Party could not have known, or greatly cared, that they were exploring the exact route of modern transportation. Nevertheless, the verdict of history is a remarkable tribute to the doggedness with which those leaders pressed on toward the west, following the most direct line." **Ibid.,** p. 26.

26 "On coming here our first view was like that of our friend Moses viewing the Promised Land. They could see the plains of Sacramento from the hills, and everything appeared fresh and green from the first rains (this was in November), and they thought they had found an earthly Paradise at last." Murphy Dictation, p. 3.

27 Bancroft, **Chronicles,** p. 32.

28 Elizabeth Yuba Murphy was born in December of 1844. "One day her parents tied her to the pommel of a saddle and tried to take her across the river. She was swept into the water and narrowly escaped death. After that they added a middle name Yuba and she was known as Lizzie Yuba. Lizzie Yuba was the first child born in California to

American pioneers." Robert O'Brien, "Riptides," San Francisco **Chronicle,** March 28, 1947.

29 Edmund Bray was a member of the Stevens-Murphy party. His "Memoirs of a Trip to California" tells of events at this time: ". . . the larger part of the company pressed on to the American River, leaving the rest at Donner Lake. The latter kept on however until they encamped on what the writer supposes to have been the Yuba. There they stayed a week, and a child was born in the Murphy family. Then 8 men, including the writer, pressed on before, leaving James Miller in charge of the women and children with the oxen for food and the wagons for shelter, and reaching Johnson's rancho on Bear Creek Dec. 23. A month after their arrival at Sutter's a party went back and brought in those left behind." Bancroft, **History of California,** IV, 447 f.

30 Hides were being boiled for food to the consistency of glue. R. B. Millard, **History of the San Francisco Bay Region** (San Francisco: The American Historical Society, 1924), p. 175.

31 "It is my understanding that we made the first trail over the present road travelled by the railroad, to California. Some trappers had come in over a southern route through Walker's Pass, but we made the first wagon road." Murphy Dictation, p. 2.

32 From the Humboldt Sink to the Sacramento Valley the Stevens-Murphy party broke trail for wagons and may well have been the discoverers. There is no good evidence that anyone traveled the route before 1844. Their route became the western section of the original emigrant road to California. Stewart, **The opening of the California Trail,** pp. 23-24.

NOTES ON CHAPTER III

1 "At the time I delivered my inaugural address in December, 1849, very few, if any, believed with me that our agricultural and commercial interests were greater and more commanding than our mineral resources. But time has shown the correctness of the opinion then expressed. For some years after the organization of the state government the members of the Senate and Assembly from the mining counties constituted a large majority in the legislature, and controlled the action of that body. But time has essentially changed this state of things, and has given the control to the agricultural counties and the manufacturing and commercial cities." P. H. Burnett, **Recollections and Opinions of an Old Pioneer** (New York: Appleton and Co., 1880), p. 365.

2 A square league by United States survey equals about seven square miles or about 4,400 acres. In the summer of 1840, Sutter went to Monterey for citizenship papers together with a land grant of 48,000 acres. He was appointed representative of Governor Alvarado with power to administer justice on the northern frontier of California. F. R. Bechdolt, **Giants of the Old West** (New York: The Century Co., 1930), p. 189.

3 H. K. Norton, **Story of California** (Chicago: A. C. McClung and Co., 1924), p. 162.

4 Bechdolt, **op. cit.,** p. 191.

5 Caughey, **California,** pp. 188-190.

6 J. A. Sutter, **New Helvetia Diary** (San Francisco: The Grabhorn Press, 1939), p. xi.

7 By the revolution of 1844-45, Californians against Mexicans, the virtual independence of California was accomplished before the American conquest. Hunt, **California and Californians,** I, 537.

8 Bancroft, **Chronicles,** p. 36. "They went to Sutter's fort and Sutter told them that Michel Torreno [sic] had been appointed governor of California, and that the native Californians were feeling very hostile towards newcomers and that it would be necessary for them to stand in with the governor. They immediately organized a company and with Sutter they marched down to Santa Clara and there found Torreno." Murphy Dictation, p. 3.

9 Bancroft, **History of California,** IV, 486 f. It is possible that while on this trek south the Murphys noted desirable sites and later procured them. "Torreno told them to return and bring the rest out and that he would give them grants of land wherever they desired." Murphy Dictation, p. 3.

10 Micheltorena abdicated to Pio Pico following the bloodless battle of Cahuenga, February 20, 1845. From then on Mexico's hold on California was nebulous. Caughey, **op. cit.,** p. 197. Several of the Murphy party assisted Micheltorena. **San Jose Mercury,** March 8, 1944.

11 "When we bought that place on the Cosomnee [sic] river the nearest place was 18 miles away, and that was Sutter's Fort." Murphy Dictation, p. 6. The title to this ranch was in James Murphy's name, probably because his father was unable to read or write. This information from the descendants of the Murphy family; notes on interviews in possession of Mr. R. R. Stuart, University of the Pacific, Stockton, California.

12 The first overt act by Americans against the Mexican government of California occurred June 10, 1846 at the Murphy Ranch. This movement, though sometimes spoken of as a turning point in California destiny, was actually shorn of much of its importance by the outbreak of the Mexican War. Tradition, however, has given it a significance which cannot be ignored. In May of 1959 the State Historical Landmarks Commission approved and registered Landmark No. 680, the site of Murphy's Ranch. There is no question about the capture of the horses having taken place at Murphy's Ranch. The "Diary" of Johann August Sutter has an entry for June 10: "A party of Americans under command of E. Merritt, took all the horses from Arce at Murphey's [sic]." "Application for Registration of Historical Points of Interest," Department of Parks and Registration, Sacramento, California. (See Appendix 1.)

13 The Arce "Memorias" states that it was at first the intention to kill him and his companions, and that they were saved only by the intercession of Murphy and his wife. Bancroft, **History of California**, V, 108 f. "Lieutenant Arci [sic] who was camped at our house with a band of horses was surprised and captured without resistance. They were going to take all the horses away when father said that the men had better be given a horse each in order that they might return to their homes, which was done." Murphy Dictation, p. 5.

14 The American settlers claimed that the General (Castro) only wanted these horses to enable the soldiers to drive the foreigners out of the Valley of the Sacramento and to burn their wheat which they said Castro had hired the wild Indians to do. T. Larkin, **Larkin Papers (1846)** (Berkeley: University of California Press, 1955), Vol. V, p. 51.

15 "Father at once began farming on the land in the Sacramento Valley while we lived there, securing seed from Santa Clara and raising wheat. He raised the first wheat raised in the Sacramento Valley." Murphy Dictation, p. 4.

16 Between January, 1846 and May, 1848 about thirty-five entries in Sutter's **Diary** refer to Martin Murphy or his rancho produce brought in to Sutter's fort. The **Diary** was a daily record kept at the fort from September 9, 1845 to May, 1848. It deals chiefly with the arrival and departure of employees, visitors, and immigrants and it is of great value as a record of exact dates, as a source of information about hundreds of early pioneers, and as a contemporary journal of local affairs. Bancroft, **History of California**, V, 616.

17 Sutter, **op. cit.**, pp. xiii, xiv.

18 J. M. Guinn, **History of the State of California** (Chicago: Chapman Publishing Co., 1904), p. 428.

19 Murphy Papers. The document locates the lots between 25th and 26th Streets extending for two blocks from L to N. A modern map of Sacramento indicates their nearness to Sutter's original property. Date of purchase: January 18, 1849. The deed for the second property bears the signature of John A. Sutter, Sr. Date of purchase: April 24, 1849.

20 Murphy Papers. This land was originally bought by Martin Murphy for $3,500 from Louis T. Sajit, May 9, 1850. The lease granted to the California Stage Company bears the date July 7, 1854 and is signed by

James Birch, President of the California Stage Company. John Watson signed for Martin Murphy, Jr.

In midsummer of 1849, James Birch established what was probably the the first stage line in California. From 1854 onward the California Stage Company operated a profitable statewide integrated service. This firm grew out of a merger of five local lines eventually running stages over routes 1,500 miles in length. Miners anxious to reach the placers in the mountains paid Birch a stage fare each way of 2 oz. of gold or $32. Caughey, **op cit.**, p. 32.

A California Historical Landmark places the first stage terminal of the 1850's on the SW corner of Front and K Streets, Sacramento.

21 San Jose **Pioneer**, Jan. 14, 1893. "We had a tutor at the Sacramento ranche [sic] by the name of Pat O'Brien, and that man used to scare me so that I could not learn my letters for six months. He was a terrific fellow, and was always looking for a fight. He would go out and pick a fight with the Indians when he could not find anyone else. He afterwards joined Walker's expedition and was killed." Murphy dictation, p. 13.

22 "Soon many of his old friends and neighbors joined him and a thriving Irish settlement grew up around him [Martin Murphy, Sr.] His home was the center to which all newcomers self-exiled from Erin turned while seeking a haven for themselves. There they found the whole-souled welcome of truly hospitable hearts, and kindly care overtaken by sickness." Article written by Marcella Fitzgerald, granddaughter of Martin Murphy, Jr., "Irish Pioneers of California: Martin Murphy, Sr.," **The Monitor**, Aug. 24, 1901.

No one was excluded from the Murphys' kindness and the Indians returned it in a unique way. The story is told that "they [the Murphys'] were never bothered during Indian uprisings because the squaws would come and sleep across the doors of the house so the braves would not attack this family." Letter received from Mrs. Frank R. Stockton, great-granddaughter of Martin Murphy, Jr., June 5, 1968.

23 Bancroft, **History of California**, I, 108. In **Echoes of the Past about California** by General John Bidwell there is an entry entitled "Mr. Larkin's Narrative" dated November 26, 1846 which refers to the Murphy family and their rancho on the Cosumnes River. John Bidwell, **op. cit.**, p. 86.

24 Sutter, **op. cit.**, p. 50. John Charles Fremont (1813-1890) was a member of the United States Topographical Corps. Fremont played a prominent role in the conquest of California. **Dictionary of American Biography** (New York: Scribner's Sons, 1936), Vol. VII, pp. 12-23.

25 Christopher Carson (1809-1868). American scout and frontiersman known as Kit Carson. He acted as guide for Fremont's three expeditions to the West in 1842-1846. **Dictionary of American Biography**, III, 530-532.

26 Alexis Godey (1800-1889). Godey was an experienced plainsman, frontiersman, and trapper. In 1843 he joined the famous "Fremont Exploring Expedition to the West." He was a rival of Kit Carson; in difficult situations he was of incalculable value to Fremont. F. L. Latta, "Alexis

Godey in Kern County," Kern County Historical Society, Bakersfield, California, November, 1939, pp. 23-24.

27 William T. Sherman, **Memoirs** (New York: D. Appleton and Co., 1875), Vol. I, p. 31.

28 J. B. Taylor, **Eldorado or Adventures in the Path of Empire** (New York: G. P. Putnam's Sons, 1892), pp. 229-230.

29 In 1830, 500 foreigners lived in the territory of California west of the Sierra Nevada mountains. By 1846 the number increased to 1,200 and three-fourths of them were Americans. R. D. Hunt, "California in Review after a Century of American Control," **Centennial Lectures** (Washington, D. C.: Government Printing Office, 1948), p. 36.

30 Because of the slavery problem, Congress could not organize a territorial government for California. J. Ellison, "Government of California 1848-50," in **California and the Nation 1850-1869** (Berkeley: University of California Press, 1927), pp. 2-3.

31 San Francisco **Alta California, Jan. 11, 1849.** Thomas Hart Benton (1772-1858), U. S. Senator from Missouri 1821 to 1851, aided all legislation that supported the frontier settlers. **Dictionary of American Biography,** II, 210-213.

32 By 1850 the population of California had risen from 15,000 as it was in 1847, to 100,000 and the average increase for six weeks thereafter was 50,000. J. F. Davis, **California: Romantic and Resourceful** (San Francisco: A. M. Robertson, 1914), p. 13.

33 Not all squatters were scoundrels. If there was a fair assumption that a given spot was not actually included in a grant, it might even be accounted a virtue in a settler to take possession and begin its development. Hunt, **op. cit.,** II, 291. On arrival in California, settlers were found to be trespassers on soil claimed by Mexican landowners. Since Congress was urged to legislate in favor of the settlers so that tillable land could be cultivated, the Federal Government was blamed for "squatter riots" in 1850 in California. Ellison, **op. cit.,** p. 11; and J. Royce, "The Squatter Riot of '50 in Sacramento," **Overland Monthly,** ser. 2, VI (September 1855), 225-46.

34 Murphy Papers. "A True Copy" of the deed. "We sold the ranche [sic] in the Sacramento Valley with the exception of the 640 acres above mentioned, together with three thousand head of cattle for fifty thousand dollars. The gold fever made the increase in price. In 1849 a perfect flood of people came into the Sacramento valley and the price of land went up." Murphy Dictation, p. 5.

35 "We reserved 640 acres of the old place there as a souvenoir [sic], which was held until a few years ago and then, when it was covered with slicken, it was sold for a comparatively small figure." **Ibid.**

36 Sometime after March of 1845 Martin Murphy, Sr., his sons James, Daniel, and John, and his daughter Ellen moved south to the pueblo of San Jose. Mr. Murphy purchased a tract of land (8,900 A.) thirty miles south of San Jose where he made a record of success in stock-raising and ranch enterprise. The property, located on the Monterey Road between Monterey and San Francisco and entitled Rancho Ojo de Agua de la Coche, had been acquired from the Mexican grantee

Juan M. Hernandez. (The present town of San Martin developed around the site of this rancho.) The house on the highway was a stopping place for travelers and came to be known as the "21 Mile House." Mr. Murphy made this his permanent home even during the dangerous times of the Mexican War. E. T. Sawyer, **History of Santa Clara County, California** (Los Angeles: Historic Record Co., 1922), p. 908.

Bayard Taylor has an interesting entry in **Eldorado:** "They introduced me to Mr. Murphy and his daughter Ellen, both residents of the country for the last six years. Mr. Murphy, who is a native of Ireland, emigrated from Missouri, with his family in 1843. He owns nine leagues of land (40,000 acres) in the valley, and his cottage is a well-known and welcome resting-place to all the Americans in the country. During the war he remained on the ranch in company with his daughter, notwithstanding Castro's troops were scouring the country, and all other families had moved to the pueblo for protection. His three sons were at the same time volunteers under Fremont's command. Taylor, **op. cit.,** p. 126 (1850 edition).

NOTES ON CHAPTER IV

1   Foreigners, especially Americans, though subject to some restrictions, might receive these land grants as well as the citizens. The average expense to the grantee did not exceed $12. Hunt, **California and Californians,** I, 286.

2   H. S. Foote, **Pen Pictures of Santa Clara County** (Chicago: The Lewis Publishing Co., 1888), p. 76. Too often the boundary marks were inaccurate and often temporary in character. An illustration of this can be found in the following act of judicial possession of Rancho San Jose: ". . . a large oak was taken as a boundary in which was placed the head of a beef and some of its limbs chopped." Hunt, **California and Californians,** I, 291.

3   **Historical Documents of California,** Vol. III, p. 87, in Bancroft Library, University of California, Berkeley.

4   January 28, 1846, p. 88; April 7, 1846, p. 159, **ibid.**

5   Some former owners of Murphy property: Juan M. Hernandez, Ojo de la Coche rancho; Dorenzo Pineda, Canada de las Uvas; Carlos Castro, San Francisco de las Llagas; Isabel Ortega, La Polka; Mariana Castro, Pastoria de las Borregas.
There were four methods of obtaining land: 1. Purchase from the government at $2 per acre (1850); 2. 160 acres by title under the Homestead Law; 3. by preemption (taking land before it came into the market, improving it and thereby establishing the right of possession, and paying the market price); 4. by purchase from private individuals. Quigley, **The Irish in California and on the Pacific Coast,** p. 171.

6   Murphy Dictation, p. 5.

7   The word "borregas" means a ewe lamb. The title Pastoria de las Borregas means sheep pasture.

8   Murphy Dictation, **loc. cit.**

9   F. Corbett, "Primer on the California Land Grants." typed copy at College of Notre Dame, Belmont, California.

10 Other Murphy ranchos confirmed by the Land Commission were: La Polka; San Francisco de las Llagas; Canada de las Uvas; Laguna Seca. Murphy Papers.
After the acquisition of California in 1848, land grants had to be separated from public domain. Therefore Congress established a Land Commission in 1851. The Act provided for Commissioners appointed by the President to verify private land grants in California with the right of appeal by either the governor or claimant to the United States Courts. Failure on the part of the owner to present claims within a specified time resulted in forfeiture and property was thereafter considered part of the public domain. Foote, **op. cit.,** p. 76.

11 Juan B. Alvarado, Constitutional Governor of the Department of California. "Don Francisco Estrada has solicited for his personal benefit and that of his family the land known by the name of Pastoria de las Borregas . . . I have resolved to grant him the mentioned land declaring to him the ownership thereof." January 15, 1832, Murphy Papers, Copy of Deed.

12 "As heir to deceased Francisco Estrada, I say that I voluntarily cede in favor of the citizen Mariano Castro the two 'sitios' [square leagues] mentioned in this title." Buenavista, March 17, 1845, Jose Mariano Estrada. Murphy Papers. Copy of Deed in Spanish, October 17, 1849, bears the signature of William P. Hartnell, Government translator, Secretary of State's Office, Monterey, California.

13 Murphy Papers, Copy of Deed. Verified by Land Commission as correct copy in July, 1854.

14 Murphy Papers. Indenture and map provide these facts for the second purchase. Third purchase: April 14, 1854 — a strip of land "157' by 200 chains" bought for $300. Murphy Papers, Copy of Indenture.

15 Murphy Papers. Document drawn up by the United States Land Commissioners.

16 **Ibid.** Jones, Tompkins, and Strode, Attorneys in San Francisco, handled the case and brought it to conclusion. Document from the Office of the Surveyor General of the United States for California, September 8, 1860.

17 Documents among the Murphy Papers indicate the increasing value of property in this section of the state: Assessment of this property in 1866 was $57,780; in 1867, $72,225; in 1878, $337.050.

18 M. J. Gates, **Rancho Pastoria de las Borregas, Mountain View, California** (San Jose: Cottle and Murgotten, 1895), p. 2.

19 Sunnyvale Historical Society's Program distributed by the Society on the occasion of the erection of the State Historical Landmark No. 644, May 22, 1960. See Appendix 2.

20 "The house we erected on the ranche [sic] down here was I guess the first frame house put up in Santa Clara County, the buildings erected before that being adobe. Our house had been shipped around the horn, landed in San Francisco and hauled up here, and we gave a carpenter in San Francisco named Dawson, five hundred acres down here to build that house, or put it together." In 1888 Mrs. Dawson still owned the land and it was "worth from $250 to $350 per acre." Murphy Dictation, p. 5.

21 In praise of his father, Bernard related in the Dictation that "one of his strong points was his cordial reception of all. It made no difference whether it was a tramp or a millionaire." Murphy Dictation, p. 7.

22 San Francisco **Morning Call,** "Martin Murphy," Oct. 21, 1884. Hospitality was synonymous with its early days. Priests on their way from San Francisco to Mission Santa Clara used the home as a stopover. A special room was set aside for visiting church dignitaries; altars were set up downstairs, and Mass celebrated for worshippers living in the area. Sunnyvale Historical Society pamphlet.
An entry in Archbishop Alemany's journal tells of one of these occasions: Dec. 15, 1863 "Visit Murphy's where I blessed Church under the title of St. Patrick." Also visits on August 14, 1862 and May 7, 1868. Alemany Journal of Correspondence," Vol. H 15, p. 60. Archives of San Francisco, Chancery Office, San Francisco, California.

23 For the facts relating to the last days of the Murphy house, see Appendix 2.

24 M. B. Hoover, **Historic Spots in California** (Stanford: Stanford University Press, 1966), pp. 446-447.

25 "The issue probably raised more interest, caused more short tempers, and used up more time than any other single controversy in Sunnyvale's history." Sunnyvale **Daily Standard**, Dec. 26, 1961.

26 San Jose **Evening News**, May 23, 1960.

27 **Census Reports 1870-1880:** U.S. Federal Census, U.S. Government Printing Office. Martin Murphy held additional property in San Francisco valued at $100,000. "Martin Murphy, Death of a Well-Known Pioneer and Millionaire," San Francisco **Morning Call**, Oct. 21, 1884.

28 The coastal area was used by the United States Government for lighthouse purposes. Bancroft, **Chronicles**, p. 46

29 La Purissima Concepcion had been granted to Jose Gregonio and Jose Ramon in 1840 and afterwards became the property of Juana Briones Miranda whose adobe was near Mayfield in Santa Clara County. Guinn, **op. cit.**, p. 428. In Mission days this rancho had been stocked with 20,000 cattle, 15,000 sheep, and 1,000 horses and mares. W. H. Davis, **60 years in California 1831-1889** (San Francisco: A. J .Leary, 1889), p. 592. In 1878, this rancho had assessed value of $60,000. Murphy Papers.

30 Milpitas Rancho was assessed in 1866 at $8,000; in 1878, at $74,980. Murphy Papers.

31 On January 3, 1889 Santa Margarita came into the railroad picture and part of Rancho Santa Margarita was subdivided, with auction sales to promote the new town. **The Story of San Luis Obispo County** (San Luis Obispo: Title Insurance and Trust Co., n.d.), p. 30.

32 **Ibid.**, map, pp. 28-29.

33 **Ibid.**, p. 55. September 27, 1841. Granted by Governor Pro Tem Manuel Jimeno (Casarin) to Joaquin Estrada.

34 Joaquin Estrada became famous for his lavish living. He brought a circus to his rancho after it had finished performing in Santa Barbara. To Santa Margarita and to his handsome Casa de Estrada he invited guests from far and near. For two weeks he was their host. Each afternoon the circus gave a show; each evening there was dancing and the feasting was continuous. When a rodeo was held on Santa Margarita, Don Joaquin made it a time of fiesta, with open-handed hospitality and princely entertainment. Hundreds of guests watched grizzly bear and bull fights, entered their horses in races, and gathered at the barbecue pits to watch whole beeves roasted. **Ibid.**, p. 13.

35 The note was for one year at 2 per cent dated February 23, 1860. In March 1860, the Atascadero Rancho was mortgaged for $6,000. Murphy Papers.

36 Murphy Papers, July 12, 1860. Copy of Indenture.

37 Granted March 27, 1861 by J. W. Mandeville, U.S. Surveyor General for California. Map of Survey, Murphy Papers.

38 Murphy Papers, Copy of Indenture. In addition to this document for purchase, another proves the reimbursement of Peter Donahue for his part in the promissary note. The paper is signed by Peter Donahue and confirms that he relinquished "all the undivided half part" of the said note on receipt of $10,000 from Martin Murphy on May 17, 1861.

39 Murphy was noted for helping those in need and "was very proud of the fact that he never foreclosed a mortgage." Letter from Mrs. Frank R. Stockton, great-granddaughter of Martin Murphy, Jr., June 5, 1968.

40 Murphy Papers, Copy of Indenture. Former owners: William Brack; Samuel W. Haight sold Atascadero to Henry Haight for $5,500; Edward McShane sold it to Joaquin Estrada.

41 Ibid., Copy of Indenture.

42 Ibid., August 8, 1864.

43 Ibid., Copy of Indenture.

44 Ibid., Copy of Indenture. Two disastrous seasons, called the Great Drought, afflicted California from 1862 to 1864. Effects were reflected in the collapse of property values in all the cattle counties. This is probably the reason why the Rancho Asuncion, 39,000 acres, was sold for $1,000. Considering the small price paid for Rancho Asuncion, the **Census Reports** of 1870 and 1880 are remarkable, for in 1870 the rancho was valued at $100,000 and in 1880 at $200,000.

45 Myron Angel, **San Luis Obispo County History** (San Francisco: Thompson and West, 1883), p. 173.

46 **Ibid.**

47 In the 1860's the total assessment value of approximately 65,000 acres was $239,372. Murphy Papers. In 1930, about 90,000 acres had a value of $1,200,000. Robert O'Brien, Riptides," **San Francisco Chronicle,** March 28, 1947

48 Santa Margarita is the home rancho of General Murphy (Brigadier-General of the National Guard of California) and is one of the loveliest and most valuable in San Luis Obispo County. The land is chiefly devoted to grazing and cattle are numbered by thousands. In the business of cattle-raising he has been eminently successful and his property is valued at $1,200,000. The family have been equally successful and their fortune aggregates $4,000,000 the result of energy, business ability, and the opportunity of life in California. Angel, **op. cit.,** pp. 32-33.

Guinn's **History of the State of California** refers to Martin Murphy as a pioneer in stock business and credits him with importing the first Norman horses into California. Murphy's birthplace, Wexford, is a section of Ireland invaded by the Normans in the eleventh century and is recognized as being the home of the high quality horse. Wexford is also famed for the skill of its horsemen. **Official Guide to County Wexford,** Wexford Chamber of Commerce, p. 32.

NOTES ON CHAPTER V

1 Both of the Martin Murphys contributed to the growth of the Church in California. In 1854, Martin, Sr., at his own expense, erected St. Martin's Church at Martinsville; it was blessed November 12, 1854 by Archbishop Alemany. The first child baptized there was Martin's grandson, Martin J. C. Murphy. **Centennial Booklet 1965**, St. Mary's Church, Gilroy, California, p. 25.

2 Bishop Alemany arrived in San Francisco on the steamer **Columbus** on December 6, 1850. Sister Gertrude Mary Gray, "A Preliminary Survey of the Life of the Most Reverend Joseph Sadoc Alemany, O.P., First Archbishop of San Francisco" (unpublished M.A. thesis, Catholic University of America, 1943), pp. 29-30.

3 In July 1853 the Holy See acted on advice of the Council of Baltimore (1852) by dividing the vast diocese of Monterey. Monterey and the district to the south came under the jurisdiction of Bishop Thaddeus Amat; northern California became the province of San Francisco with Archbishop Alemany as the first Metropolitan. **Ibid.**, p. 34.

4 Murphy Dictation, p. 10.

5 Among the Murphy Papers is a note signed by Archbishop Alemany in receipt of $200 "alms for Masses" dated May 26, 1880. Gratitude to the Murphys was expressed in a forceful way on one occasion when he acted as witness for their property ownership. "The Archbishop is here as witness." (signed) J. A. Forbes, San Jose, April 27, 1855.

The wealth and liberality of Martin Murphy, Jr. is a well-known fact but records of specific donations to the Church and education are few. The records of St. Joseph Church, San Jose, were destroyed by fire but Mrs. Tipton says that he paid for one of the towers. "I don't believe Martin Murphy, Jr., cared about publicity or records of his contributions." Letter from Mrs. Robert C. Tipton, great-granddaughter of Martin Murphy, July, 1965.

A "List of Subscribers" to rebuild or repair a new church in Santa Cruz also proves the Murphy family's interest in church building "in every direction." Four of the five paid subscribers listed were members of the Murphy family. Murphy Papers.

6 Murphy Dictation, p. 10.

7 Father Nobili had labored for many years as a missionary among the Indians in Oregon. The mission at Santa Clara was rebuilt by 1854. Other Jesuits in the founding group were Fathers Michael Accolti, Peter De Vos, and Gregory Mangarini. E. Laveille, S.J. **Life of Father De Smet**, S.J. (Milwaukee: Bruce Publishing Co., 1940), **passim.**

8 In pursuance of that suggestion he called Father Noble [sic], the first President of the College, who had been a missionary among the Indians in Oregon, and after many struggles the present institution was founded." Murphy Dictation p. 8.

9 William R. McQuoid, letter to Hubert Howe Bancroft, MS in Bancroft Library, University of California, Berkeley. "The Murphy children were the first who attended the Santa Clara College, and in fact founded that institution . . . Before going to Santa Clara College, the Murphy boys had a private tutor at the ranche [sic] and when they went to the college they took their tutor there with them." Murphy Dictation, p. 9.

10 Joseph Dunn, **The Glories of Ireland** (Washington, D.C.: Phoenix Limited, 1914), p. 42.

11 Sister Mary Dominica McNamee, S.N.D. de N., **Willamette Interlude** (Palo Alto, Calif.: Pacific Books, 1959), p. 237.

12 Gray, **op. cit.,** p. 47.

13 San Jose became the capital of California in 1849. After meeting in San Jose and for brief periods in Vallejo and Benicia, the legislature moved to Sacramento which was established as the State Capital in 1854.

14 Murphy Dictation, p. 8.

15 J. P. Munro-Fraser, **History of Santa Clara County** (San Francisco: Alley, Bowan and Co., 1881), p. 490.

16 "The old gentleman was the founder of the convent and gave the land it occupies . . . The first children to attend the convent were my sisters." Murphy Dictation, pp. 8-9.

17 McNamee, **op. cit.,** p. 268.

18 Richard H. Dana makes reference to both institutions in the Appendix of **Two Years Before the Mast:** "Making San Francisco my headquarters, I paid visits to various parts of the state, — down the Bay to Santa Clara, with its live oaks and sycamores, and its Jesuit College for Boys; and San Jose, where is the best girls' school in the state, kept by the Sisters of Notre Dame . . ." R. H. Dana, **Two Years Before the Mast** (New York: Random House, 1936), p. 412.

19 Guinn, **A History of the State of California,** p. 428.

20 "In Memoriam" (Evelyn A. Murphy, granddaughter of Martin Murphy, Jr.), **California Historical Quarterly,** XXV (March, 1945), 89.

21 The assessed value of Pastoria de las Borregas: in 1860 it was $25,000; 1870, $80,000; 1880, $250,000. Murphy Papers.

22 "Hay and grain were the principal crops and he also raised a great many cattle. Formerly the ranche [sic] was entirely devoted to cattle, but after the country became settled up the land became too valuable for that purpose and were moved to San Luis Obispo County, and the ranche devoted entirely to grain. The ranche consisted of about 5,000 acres." Murphy Dictation, pp. 8-9. The three southern ranchos were acquired in the 1860's.

23 Statistics from the **San Jose Directory** for 1874 indicate the extent of production in this part of the state: acres of land in wheat, 172,573; bushels of wheat, 1,578,843; number of grape vines, 1,182,093; gallons per annum, 2,500,000. **San Jose Directory,** 1874, p. 198.
    Gates credits Martin Murphy for planting the first orchard in the San Jose area. Gates, **Rancho Pastoria de las Borregas,** p. 19.

24 Murphy's profit for one year in the 1850's was $60,000. Guinn, **op. cit.,** p. 428.

25 Edward D. Young, **Special Report on Immigration** (Philadelphia: M'Laughlin Brothers, 1871), p. 76. The price was the highest of all counties: $1.30 to $1.80 per cwt.

26 In one year, 1880-81, a thousand tons were insured for $20,000. Murphy Papers.

27 Bancroft, **Chronicles,** p. 46. The average yield per acre was from 2 to 3 tons. Gates, **op. cit.,** p. 24.

28 "He was a great trader and would always calculate carefully a bargain in all its aspects. If he had money he would figure out its interest: then he would figure out what could be made by putting it into cattle; and then what could be realized by putting it into land. If he bought land he would figure out as to whether he should raise cattle or wheat." Murphy Dictation, p. 8.

29 W. F. James and Geo. H. McMurray, **History of San Jose** (San Jose: A. H. Cawston Publishers, 1933), p. 86. "Father had several buildings in San Jose; he owned the present Jefferson block, the Washington block and a block on the corner of Market and Santa Clara Street." Murphy Dictation, p. 10. It was said of Martin Murphy that no one had ever seen his signature to either a deed or a mortgage. He bought but he never sold. "Subdivision of Estate," **The Wave**, Vol. 9, No. 12, Sept. 17, 1892.

30 "My first remembrance of Santa Clara County is that there were very few adobe houses here in town. I don't suppose over twenty-five or thirty of any size. There were no brick buildings in town." Murphy Dictation, P. 9.

31 F. Hall, **History of San Jose** (San Francisco: A. L. Bancroft and Co., 1871), p. 276. These were built in 1858. In March of 1868, more brick buildings on the south side of Santa Clara Street were constructed by Murphy and used as city stables. Foote. **op. cit.**, p. 140.

32 This was the last location of the court house prior to the construction of a new building. The first Supreme Court of California State was held at Murphy's large hall at the corner of Market and Eldorado Streets. The rent was $190 per month. **Ibid.**

33 Murphy Papers. Martin Murphy's certificate of citizenship is dated November 1, 1855.

34 **Historical Documents**, Table 269. Bancroft Library, University of California, Berkeley.

35 "Poll Lists of the Election Districts of the County of Santa Clara 1867-1879." Murphy is also registered in the following years: 1873, 1875, 1876, and 1879 in the Santa Clara County Records, California State Library, Sacramento.

36 The Society was organized in 1850 and, according to its constitution, was designed to be "A Moral, Benevolent, Literary, and Scientific Association." It was exclusive, admitting to senior membership only those who had arrived in California before the end of 1849. It was affluent, with assets totaling almost half a million dollars. J. W. Caughey, **Hubert Howe Bancroft** (Berkeley: University of California Press, 1946), p. 341. Martin Murphy's certificate of membership is in the Register for the Society. **Register for the Society of California Pioneers** (San Francisco: Society of California Pioneers), p. 171.

37 Frank Soule **et al., Annals of San Francisco** (New York: D. Appleton and Co., 1855), p. 822. Other members of the Murphy family who were members of the California Pioneer Society by 1880 were: James Murphy, Bernard Murphy, James T. Murphy, Mrs. Martin Murphy, W. B. Murphy, Daniel T. Murphy, and John M. Murphy.

38 Murphy Dictation, p. 11.

39 The San Jose **Weekly Patriot** was started by F. B. Murdoch in 1863. J. B. Hewson, **Directory of the City of San Jose** (San Francisco: Bacon and Company, 1874), p. 44.

40 Murphy Dictation, p. 11. During the two decades following the establishment of state government in California, people had a lukewarm interest in national affairs and little or no knowledge of the workings of state government. Two of Murphy's sons were among the energetic men who had concern for California's future. Patrick W. represented San Luis Obispo, Ventura, and Santa Barbara counties in the State Senate during 1865-68 and again in 1878. Bernard D. was a member of the Assembly in 1868 and of the Senate in 1877 representing Santa Clara County. He was elected Mayor of San Jose in 1878. Bancroft, **History of California,** IV, 748-750.

41 Murphy Dictation, p. 7.

42 Work on the Central Pacific Railroad began at Sacramento in 1863, and a San Francisco and San Jose Railroad was opened for operation. A. F. Rolle, **California** (New York: Thomas Y. Crowell Co., 1963), p. 321.

43 "Release of Right of Way to the San Francisco and San Jose Railroad," July 27, 1861. Murphy Papers. "Father's ranche [sic] lies between Mountain View and Laurel Station about ten miles from here between here and San Francisco. The Southern Pacific road passes through it." Murphy Dictation, pp. 8-9.

44 Munro-Fraser, **History of Santa Clara County,** p. 539.

45 Note signed by Haynes and Bothwell, contractors by Theodore Lenzen, Architect, October 1, 1870. Murphy Papers.

46 Bancroft, **Chronicles,** p. 48.

47 San Francisco **Morning Call,** Aug. 30, 1892.

48 Documents show that money was lent to the Estudillo family who owned the San Leandro Rancho in Alameda County, California. Murphy Papers (Appendix 6).

49 The commercial rate for banks at that time was 3 per cent. While Martin, Sr. charged no interest on his loans which totaled $25,000 from 1849 to 1856, Martin, Jr. charged 1½ per cent on a total of $50,000 from 1851 to 1857. The money-lending practices of the Murphys are exceptional. Murphy Papers.

In the 1850's interest rates from 2 to 10 per cent a month, compounded, were customarily charged even on amply secured loans. R. G. Cleland, **From Wilderness to Empire** (New York: Alfred A. Knopf, 1959), p. 137.

50 Notes of acknowledgment from Archbishop Alemany and the Sisters of the Holy Family in San Francisco are among the Murphy Papers.

Mrs. Robert Tipton, great-granddaughter of Martin Murphy, Jr., states in a letter received in July 1965 that it is probable that many of Murphy's benefactions went unrecorded because he did not want the publicity for what he did.

51 Murphy Dictation, p. 7.

52 Program for the erection of the Sunnyvale Historical Landmark No. 644 on the site of Murphy's home. (Appendix 2)

53 See Appendix 7 for the reprint of this article.

54 Mary Bolger Murphy was also well-known for her excellent qualities of character and together they established the family tradition of Catholicity, social awareness coupled with generosity, hospitality, and benefactions to those in need. Mrs. Murphy was, I believe, one of the most benevolent and kindly women in California. She was the incarnation of sympathy, charity, and generosity. Incapable of anger or of harboring a resentment, she might have been regarded as too good-natured and indulgent if it were not for her innate shrewdness, her unerring sagacity, and her fine industry and thrift . . . Considering her endless good deeds and her boundless hospitality it is no wonder that her death is so mourned by her family and her countless friends." **The Wave,** Vol. 9, No. 12, Sept. 17, 1892.

55 The collection of letters among the Murphy Papers includes those received from Archbishop Alemany and the California State Governor, George Perkins. (Appendix 7)

56 "Death of a Pioneer of Pioneers," Sacramento **Union,** Oct. 21, 1884.

57 "The peculiarity of my father's distribution was that he and my mother, when the old gentleman found that he had not much longer to live, joined in a deed distributing the property equally among all the children, sons and daughters share and share alike, simply reserving a life interest of the rents and profits. In that way all the expenses of probate and partition were avoided, as he designated the land each should occupy." Murphy Dictation, p. 11. Details concerning the Will are in Appendix 8.

58 Sacramento **Daily Bee,** Oct. 22, 1884.

59 San Francisco **Morning Call,** Oct. 21, 1884. Subtitle for the article was "A large fortune deeded away to avoid risks of law." The reference to shifting occupations and gambling speculations" highlights the fact that Murphy adhered strictly to his occupation as a farmer and cattle-breeder during the days of goldmining speculation. He resisted the "glittering temptation of multiplied profits" and could be contented with the "slow but steady gains of legitimate business." San Francisco **Morning Call,** Aug. 30, 1892.

60 Reprint of an article in the San Jose **Pioneer,** Jan. 14, 1893. This article appeared in the 90th anniversary edition of the **Santa Clara Journal,** 1962.

61 Other participants in the ceremony were: Father Aloysius Bixio, S.J., Deacon; Father Bartholomew Calzia, S.J., Sub-deacon; Father Nicholas Congiato, S.J., Assistant priest; Mr. Butner, Master of Ceremonies. The pallbearers were: David Belden, F. E. Spencer, T. W. Spring, Muriane Malarin, B. P. Rankin, E. McLaughlin, P. De Saisset, James Enright, C. T. Ryland, William Dunphy. San Jose **Pioneer,** Jan. 14, 1893.

62 **Ibid.** Martin Murphy's son Bernard gave the following tribute to his father: "He was a man who never spoke ill of anybody and never mentioned his neighbors except in a kindly way. If the course of any neighbor was not right he always had an excuse for him. I never in my life heard him speak unkindly of any body." Murphy Dictation, p. 7.

63 San Francisco **Morning Call,** Oct. 21, 1884.

64 San Jose **Pioneer,** Jan. 14, 1893.

APPENDIX 1

California Landmark No. 680 on Martin Murphy, Jr.'s Ranch on the Cosumnes River, Sacramento County, California.

In May of 1959 the State Historical Landmarks Commission and the State Park Commission approved and registered as a State Historical Landmark No. 680 the site of Murphy's Ranch which is located west of the Stockton to Sacramento road on the north bank of the Cosumnes River. The registration of this Landmark was requested and supported by the California History Foundation of the University of the Pacific, the Stockton Corral of Westerners, and the Sacramento Historical Society.

The first overt act by Americans against the government of California by Mexico occurred on June 10, 1846 at the Murphy Ranch. This movement, though sometimes spoken of as a turning point in California destiny, was actually shorn of much of its importance by the outbreak of the Mexican War. Tradition, however, has given it a significance which cannot be ignored. To the popular mind, this uprising will probably always stand as the embodiment of pioneer spirit and the decisive stroke by which California was saved to the United States.

With reference to the initial act of the Bear Flag Revolt at Murphy's Ranch, an article in the *Pacific Historian* states:

As Dr. McIntosh points out in a lead article of this issue of the **Historian,** the conquest of this Mexican province, and the acquisition of the area by the United States was set in motion elsewhere; it was to be one of the fruits of the war against Mexico and the skirmishes and pronouncements, and flag-making by Americans in California were unnecessary to this purpose. Unknown to anyone in California, war against Mexico had been declared by the Congress of the United States almost a month earlier on May 13. But as Dr. McIntosh also implies, these rebellious actions were significant in the pattern of American Mexican relationships. The site of this first act of force against the Mexican government is one of the more important historic landmarks in California. It would undoubtedly have been registered and marked long before now but for the difficulty of locating the "Murphy Ranch."[1]

Mr. Reginald R. Stuart of the California Historical Foundation was able to establish the facts necessary for the registration of this landmark. The first owner of the tract of land was Ernest Rufus; maps of the early 1840's designate the area as "Rancho de Ernesto."[2] In his Dictation, Bernard Murphy tells of Martin Murphy, Jr.'s purchase of this land in 1845:

My father settled in the Sacramento Valley about 18 miles this side of where the city now is, on the Mocosome [sic] River, now called the Cosomnee [sic] River, on two leagues of land for which he paid $250.[3]

In the corral of this ranch, Lieutenant Francisco Arce placed the army horses which he was driving from the Sonoma Valley to the San Jose area. The first participants in the revolt consisted of a handful of landholders in the Sacramento Valley, and a somewhat larger number of hunters and trappers from the same region.[4] When the band of American settlers, few in number, conferred with Captain John C. Fremont, overcame Lieutenant Arce,[5] and then captured the horses and drove them back up the Sacramento Valley to the American settlements, they committed themselves to rebellion against the Mexican government.

On May 28, 1850, Martin Murphy sold one-half of his Cosumnes holdings to Burt Holcomb, Adolphus W. Ingalsbe, John L. Scoggin, and Andrew Chambers for $50,000.[6] The section was "three miles in length from North to South, by twelve miles in length from East to West."

. . . lying and being in the county of Sacramento and State of California. Known as the Cosesmey [sic] Ranch, and bounded as follows — On the North by the Public Domain or unoccupied lands — On the East by land which Martin Murphy purchased from one Sheldon — On the South by the margin of the Cosesmay [sic] River — On the West by the Toolies [sic] or swamp — the Easterly and Westerly lines of said premises extend three miles in length from North to South.[7]

The ranch changed ownership several times since Murphy lived there. At one time the land was owned by Thomas McConnell and many people still refer to it as the McConnell Ranch. Mr. Jack Lewis was the owner in 1959 and gave permission for its registration as an historical landmark.

A plaque was erected on the west side of Highway 99 in the fall of 1959 with an appropriate ceremony. The inscription on the plaque reads as follows:

MURPHY RANCH

This is the site of the beginning of the Conquest of California by the United States. On June 10, 1846, American settlers led by Ezekial Merritt overpowered the soldiers under Lieutenant Francisco Arce and took their Mexican army horses from the corral of the Murphy Ranch on the north

bank of the Cosumnes River. The "Bear Flag" action in Sonoma followed on
June 14, 1846.
California Registered Historical Landmark No. 680. Plaque placed by Cali-
fornia Historical Foundation of the College of the Pacific and the Stockton
Corral of Westerners, October 17, 1959.[8]

1   Glenn Price, "Murphy's Ranch — New State Landmark," The Pacific
    Historian, May, 1959, p. 30.
2   Murphy Paper. Document gives names of property holders adjacent to
    Murphy's Cosumnes Ranch. One portion of the ranch was purchased
    from Jared Sheldon.
3   Murphy Dictation, p. 3.
4   R. G. Cleland, A History of California (New York: The Macmillan
    Co., 1939), p. 194.
5   Arce "Memorias" says that it was at first the intention to kill him and
    his companions, and that they were saved only by the intercession of
    Murphy and his wife. Bancroft. History of California, V. 108 f. Fre-
    mont ordered seizure of the Mexican horses from Lieutenant Arce.
    R. D. Hunt, John Bidwell, Prince of California Pioneers (Caldwell, Idaho:
    Caxton Printers, 1942), p. 129.
6   Murphy Papers. The copy of the Indenture gives the sale price for
    the rancho.
7   Murphy Papers, Copy of Indenture.
8   Price, op. cit., p. 30. This erection of Landmark No. 680 was sponsored
    by the Sacramento Historical Society.

APPENDIX 2

*California Landmark No. 644 on the Murphy Estate, Sunnyvale,
California.*

In January of 1954 an article in the San Jose *Mercury* announced that the "105-year-old Martin Murphy, Jr. house" at 252
North Sunnyvale Avenue was to be designated as a city or state
monument and preserved for posterity. Its value was estimated at
$100,000.[1] Five years later, 1959, plans were publicized regarding
the Santa Clara County Festival of Arts to be held May 3 to promote the establishment of a public and historical center in Sunnyvale. The Murphy Estate was the site chosen for the festival.[2]

In order to influence public opinion, the San Jose *Mercury*
reprinted an article describing the origin of the house and some of
its interesting aspects:

Martin Murphy built the Murphy house late in 1849 of lumber, partly
prefabricated and shipped around the Horn from Bangor, Maine. There were
no nails available so the house was doweled with wooden pegs. Beams are
tied together with rawhide thongs. After one hundred years there is no
evidence of decay. Original furniture was shipped by Martin, Jr. from New

Orleans. It is in the French style of the Napoleonic era of the very early 1800's

. . . black walnut, oval dining table; two pianos, a grand square of undetermined date made by Derker Bros., New York. The other one, smaller, made by Mussard Freres, Paris, France; dated 1855 and bearing imprint of a medal won in an 1849 exposition. Shipped around Horn.

In the "Bishop's Room" — a magnificent bedstead; headpiece 6 ft. high and elaborately scrolled.[3]

As a means of forwarding this project, additional steps were taken in the State Legislature by Mr. Clark Bradley, Republican Assemblyman from San Jose. Mr. Bradley proposed the Assembly Bill No. 1348 authorizing the state to acquire the Murphy home as an historical monument.[4] An alternative move contemplated by authorities in Sunnyvale was to make the home "a gift to the state by the city of Sunnyvale which owns it."[5] The efforts of Mr. Bradley and his assistants were successful and Governor Brown signed Bill No. 1348.[6]

On Sunday, May 22, 1960, the city of Sunnyvale sponsored a dedication ceremony and erection of State Historical Landmark Plaque No. 644 for the twenty-room, two-story Martin Murphy home. An article in the San Jose *Evening News* spoke hopefully of the restoration of the old homestead: "The four acres and house, all that's left of the 4,000 acres once owned by the Irish immigrant, eventually will be restored — when the state has funds."[7]

Even before the erection of the plaque, debates continued within the Sunnyvale City Council regarding the problem of restoration. Since the acquisition of the property by the city, public opinion had been strong on both sides of the question — "To demolish the structure or to rebuild it."[8]

When purchased in 1954, the plan was to make the home a monument to the city's history. As years passed, however, termites and fire (1958) brought severe damage to the building and renovation would have been costly.

It was through the efforts of members of the Sunnyvale Historical Society that the Murphy property reached the status of a State Historical Landmark. This group of enterprising people went further and roused the interest of the State Division of Beaches and Parks in the preservation of the home. After a preliminary investigation, the state offered to spend as much as $78,000 to renovate the building if the city would donate the land to the state and then maintain and operate the site as a part of the state system of historical monuments. A second investigation brought the cost of renewal to $200,000. Cost of maintenance and operation thereafter by the city of Sunnyvale would have been between $30,000 and $50,000 per year. The City Councilmen rejected the state's proposal.[9]

The decision to raze the historical structure did not come easily to the members of the Sunnyvale City Council, yet the ravages of progress did not spare this relic of California history. The order for demolition of the 111-year-old home came at a Council meeting on September 28, 1961, bulldozers did the work of devastation while the hopeful members of the Sunnyvale citizenry worked to influence public opinion. All that remains today is the bronze plaque proclaiming the site as Landmark No. 644 in the history of California. The inscription reads as follows:

1 San Jose **Mercury**, Jan. 13, 1954.
2 **Ibid.**, April 2, 1959.
3 San Jose **Mercury**, June 17, 1951.
4 **Sunnyvale Historical Society Bulletin**, August, 1959. Leader of the movement to preserve the historic Murphy home was the Sunnyvale Historical Society which was formed and incorporated as a non-profit society when the City Council threatened the home's demolition.
5 San Jose **Mercury**, July 21, 1959.
6 A short time after this achievement, a Sunnyvale City Councilman questioned how deeply committed the City was to turning the property over to the state and suggested that the property be sold and library books purchased. **Sunnyvale Historical Society Bulletin**, August, 1959.
7 San Jose **Evening News**, May 23, 1960.
8 "Murphy House Is Gone," Sunnyvale **Daily Standard**, Dec. 26, 1961.
9 **Ibid.**

HOME OF MARTIN MURPHY, JR.

Martin Murphy, Jr. arrived in California with his family in 1844 in the first wagon train to cross the Sierra Nevada. The founder of Sunnyvale, he constructed here his house of pre-fabricated lumber, brought around the Horn in 1849. Members of the Murphy family lived here continuously until 1953, when the property was acquired by the city of Sunnyvale.
California Registered Historical Landmark No. 644. Plaque placed by the California State Park Commission in co-operation with the city of Sunnyvale and the Sunnyvale Historical Society. May 22, 1960.

APPENDIX 3

Murphy Family Chronology

I. Martin Murphy, Sr. 1785-1865 m. Mary Foley c. 1788-1843.
   Children born in Ireland:
      1. Martin Murphy, Jr. 1807-1884 m. Mary Bolger 1808-1892
      2. James Murphy 1809-1888 m. Ann Martin 1821-1900

3. Margaret Murphy 1811-1881 m. Thomas Kell 1804-1878 (d. 1853?)
4. Johanna Murphy 1813-1899 m. Patrick Fitzgerald 1800-1849
5. Mary Murphy 1816-1882 m. James Miller 1813-1890
6. Bernard Murphy (Brian) 1815-1853 m. Catherine O'Toole 1828-1925 (2nd husband James Dunne)

Children born in Canada:

7. Ellen Murphy 1822-1895 m. Charles M. Weber 1814-1881
8. John M. Murphy 1824-1892 m. Virginia Reed 1833-1921
9. Daniel Murphy 1826-1882 m. Mary Fisher 1836-1902 (2nd husband Peter J. Colombet)

II. Martin Murphy, Jr. 1807-1884 m. Mary Bolger 1808-1892

Children born in Canada:

1. James Murphy 1832-1852
2. Martin J. Murphy 1836-1865 m. Susan Maguire c. 1840- c. 1896 (2nd husband [?] Lowe)
3. Patrick W. Murphy 1838-1901 m. Mary Catherine O'Brien 1847-1875
4. Bernard D. Murphy 1841-1911 m. Anna Lucy McGoeghegan 1851-1902

Children born in California:

5. Elizabeth Yuba Murphy 1844-1875 m. William P. Taaffe c. 1838-c. 1871
6. Mary Ann Murphy 1847-1934 m. Richard T. Carroll 1845-1890
7. Ellen Genevieve Murphy 1849-1916 m. Joaquin R. Arques 1843-1882
8. James T. Murphy 1852-1898 m. Wilhelmina Mary Dawson 1849-1914
Three children died in infancy: Mary and Nellie in Quebec; Ann Elizabeth in Missouri.

APPENDIX 4

Murphy "Firsts"

Some of the "firsts" may, of course, be removed by future investigation, but up to the beginning of 1968 the following list of "firsts" stands in California tradition:

A. As to the Murphy group:

1. First to cross the Sierra Nevada Mountains into California via the Truckee River and Donner Lake route, a route later used in the building of the Transcontinental Railroad. P. T. Hanna, **California Through Four Centuries**, p. 74. (See bibiliography for other data on this and following references.)
2. First emigrant group to bring wagons over the mountain pass into California. John Bidwell, **Echoes of the Past About California**, edited by M. Quaife, p. 86.
3. First group to bring American cattle into California. E. T. Sawyer, **History of Santa Clara County**, p. 908.
4. First of the overland emigrants to enter California by way of the Truckee River route. Hanna, **op. cit.**, p. 74.

5. First of the emigrants into California to reach Lake Tahoe and the lake afterwards called Donner. G. R. Stewart, **The California Trail,** p. 71.

B. As to Martin Murphy, Jr., himself:

1. His daughter, Elizabeth Yuba, born in December of 1844 was the first child born of emigrant parents in California. R. D. Hunt, **California Firsts,** p. 285.
2. First school in the Sacramento County was conducted by Patrick O'Brien acting as tutor to the Murphy children. H. H. Bancroft, **Chronicles of the Builders of the Commonwealth,** p. 44.
3. First overt act against the Mexican government occurred on the Murphy's Cosumnes River Rancho. "Diary" of John A. Sutter.
4. First successful wheat farming in the Sacramento Valley was achieved by Murphy. Murphy Dictation, p. 4.
5. First frame house in the Santa Clara Valley was built on the Murphy's rancho. Murphy Dictation, p. 5.
6. First Supreme Court in California was established on his property in San Jose. R. B. Millard, **History of the San Francisco Bay Region,** p. 175.
7. First Norman horses imported into California. J. M. Guinn, **History of the State of California,** p. 428.
8. First farm machinery brought from the east via Panama and used in the Santa Clara Valley. Murphy Dictation, p. 8.
9. First orchards planted in the Santa Clara Valley. M. J. Gates, "Rancho Pastoria de la Borregas, Mountain View, California," p. 19.
10. First brick buildings in San Jose. Murphy Dictation, p. 9.

APPENDIX 5

Letter of William R. McQuoid to Hubert Howe Bancroft regarding the biography of Martin Murphy, Jr. included in Bancroft's *Chronicles of the Builders of the Commonwealth.*

San Jose Cal
Sept 13th 1888

H. H. Bancroft
 My Dear Sir:
 I desire to call your attention to a few points in connection with the Murphy biography. The biography is to be of Martin Murphy Jun [sic] deceased and his children. Martin is to be made the central figure[.] In considering Martin Murphy Jun you have truly a great man to work on. The biography should be truthful and still prepard [sic] in a way that will be pleasing[.]
 They crossed the plains in 1844, coming in advance of the Donner party, therefore make the trip prominent by reason of its being the very earliest of white immigrants — Make Martin Murphy Jun conspicuous as an early pioneer and an empire builder[.]
 The Murphy family left Missouri, for the principal reason, that the religious and educational advantages were not of a pleasing character, and came to

Cal because it was a Catholic country — Martin Murphy Jun was much devoted to his church and religious duty, contributing largely to the support of the Catholic church. His boys were the first to enter the Santa Clara College at Santa Clara Cal. and by his patronage and liberality he became in a large measure the founder of that great institution[.]

His daughters were likewise the first to enter Notre Dame College at San Jose Cal, and by his patronage and liberality he became in a large measure the founder of that great institution[.] His religious character wants to be brought out strong and prominent — All through his Cal life there was an innate something, that induced him to keep an open house and free table for all the strangers and poor people passing through the country. That custom has been religiously continued since his death, at his old ranch, near Mountain View[.] It was known far and near the character of the house kept by Martin Murphy, and for thirty five years, he, and his family after him, have distributed charity in that way, feeding from one to fifteen persons every meal during all that time.

No man was ever charged for meals or lodging at his ranch. No man was ever refused the hospitality of his table — This custom in life, taken in connection with the great feast given on the occasion of his "golden wedding", the magnitude of which was never equalled on the Pacific Coast, will enable you to bring out, in thrilling colors, a very commendable trait of character. The people all had the greatest respect and the fullest confidence in him as a man. He exemplified in life all the commendable virtues of a truly good and great man[.]

No sham or hipocracy [sic] in his make up — He was a great and successful business man, and a proper reference to his financial success would not be displeasing to his family — There should be a proper reference made to Martin Murphy Sen. There should be an **appropriate** notice given of Mrs. Martin Murphy Jun, who is still living[.]

We were given very little information regarding the daughters of Martin Murphy Jun, and consequently very little can be said regarding them[.]

Martin Murphy Jun had five sons — James and Martin S. are dead, and the day on which James died another son was born who was also given the name of James. There cannot be much said of James, but in addition to what appears in the dictation, he has only recently completed a very extensive trip around the world, visiting all points of historic note in the old world[.]

Gen. Patrick W. has attained quite a prominence in public life. In addition to the dictation, a sketch of his life appears in the county history of San Louis [sic] Obrofo [sic] County[.]

I herewith call your attention to the history of Santa Clara County by Alley Bowden [sic] and Co., in which appears the biographies of Martin Murphy Sen (page 724) Hon B. D. Murphy (page 723) and Martin Murphy Jun (page 791) [.]

In giving the dictation B. D. Murphy referred to the above biographies, and said so far as they went, they were thought to be correct[.]

Please remember that the Hon B. D. Murphy is the person who we especially want to please. In addition to the dictation and biography cited, he is now a candidate on the Cleveland ticket for elector at large, having been nominated without any knowledge or effort on his part[.]

He is the business successor of his father. By unanimous consent he is said to be just like his father in liberality and manly principles[.]

I want you to say as little as possible about the brothers and sisters of Martin Murphy Jun — Let whatever may be said, be of a complimentary character, but give them no special prominence — I think I have fully touched on the special matters to be considered. With kindly greeting I remain.

Very respectfully
W. R. McQuoid

P.S. Martin Murphy Sen born Jan 1st 1785 and died March 16th 1865 Martin Murphy Jun born Nov 9th 1807 and died Oct. 20th 1884.

APPENDIX 6

Partial List of Documents Among Murphy Papers

Tax Receipts: City of San Jose

		Assessment	Tax
1.	11/21/1864	$ 51,000	$ 510
2.	6/ 7/1877	117,000	1,053

Tax Receipts: County of Santa Clara

| 1. | 11/17/1866 | $142,680 | $3,324.44 |
| 2. | 1/ 7/1878 | 440,310 | 7,044 |

Indentures:

1. 1/15/1842   Pastoria de las Borregas; Juan Bautista Alvarado to Francisco Estrada.
2. 3/17/1845   Pastoria de las Borregas; Jose Estrada to Mariano Castro.
3. 4/24/1849   Sacramento City lots; John Augustus Sutter to Martin Murphy, Jr.
4. 5/ 8/1850   Sale of rancho on the Cosumnes River; Martin Murphy, Jr. to Burt Holcomb **et al.** $50,000.
5. 9/17/1850   First document referring to the purchase of Pastoria de las Borregas; Mariano Castro to Martin Murphy, Jr. Murphy cedes this property to Mary, his wife, before taking a "long and dangerous" journey.
6. 1/ 8/1851   First purchase of Pastoria de las Borregas from Mariano Castro; $12,500 for 3,207-¼ A.
7. 1/10/1851   Mary Murphy cedes property to Martin Murphy; Journey to "Atlantic states and Canada" cancelled.
8. 5/ 1/1851   Second purchase from Mariano Castro; $5,000 for 1,688-½ A.
9. 5/14/1854   Third purchase from Mariano Castro. Rather than move the fence, Murphy bought the strip of land for $300.
10. 7/27/1854   Lease of Sacramento lot to James Birch, President of the California Stage Company.
11. 5/18/1858   Contract for erecting the brick buildings in San Jose; agreement with John McDermott.

Loans: (2% rate of interest)

1849	$8,608
1851	$3,294; $600
1854	$196; $3,977; $10,000
1856	$10,000; $14,000
1857	$2,500; $600; $1,000; $11,000; $6,000; $500
1858	$1,000; $2,000
1864	$977

Mortgages (includes purchase of property):

1. 2/ 9/1859 $35,000 on San Leandro property of the Estudillo family.
2. 12/ 1/1859 $12,500 on same No. 2.
3. 2/23/1860 $20,000 on Santa Margarita Rancho owned by Joaquin Estrada (shared with Peter Donahue of S. F.).
4. 3/23/1860 $6,000 on Rancho Atascadero owned by Joaquin Estrada.
5. 7/12/1860 $5,000 on Santa Margarita and Atascadero Ranchos owned by Joaquin Estrada.
6. 4/ 8/1861   Sale of Santa Margarita Rancho by Joaquin Estrada to Martin Murphy, Jr. for $45,000.
7. 5/17/1861 $10,000 to Peter Donahue; Murphy assumes the $20,000 mortgage on Santa Margarita Rancho.
8. 10/ 3/1864   Purchase of Asuncion by Murphy from William Farrell; 11 square leagues for $1,000.
9. 10/ 8/1864   Purchase of rights on Atascadero from Goldtree and Cohen by P. W. Murphy, $4,750.
10. 10/12/1864   Purchase of Atascadero from Goldtree and Cohen.

Maps:

1. 10/13/1853   rancho of Mariano Castro.
2. (No Date)   Pastoria de las Borregas.
3.   1852   sketch shows the Three Purchases which Murphy made from Mariano Castro for Pastoria de las Borregas confines.

Other documents related to land claims:

1. Martin Murphy, Jr. made an agreement with Jones, Tompkins, and Strode and promised an extra $500 for confirmation of Pastoria de las Borregas. S. F., Aug. 9, 1852.
2. July 5, 1854, Board of Land Commissioners' decree of confirmation for Pastoria de las Borregas; Case No. 257.
3. Opinion of the Board of Land Commissioners regarding the land belonging to Ynigo, the Indian who was living on Pastoria de las Borregas, 12/19/1857.
4. 3/17/1857. Bill for $1,000 for the survey of Las Llagas, La Polka, Ojo de la Coche, Las Uvas, and Laguna Seca. Receipt by Richard P. Hammond and A. W. Thompson.

5. 7/9, 13, 30/1858. Settlement for Rancho del Refugio which was Mariano Castro's rancho adjacent to that of Murphy. This is one of the documents which bears Murphy's "mark" +.

6. 4/27/1859. Washington, D.C., Department of the Interior **re** the land of Ynigo on Pastoria de las Borregas.

Miscellaneous Documents:

1. 1/25/1845. Promissory note to Elisha Stevens for $75. signed by Dennis Martin.

2. Order from J. Bidwell for olive cuttings to be sent to Chico. Signature of John Bidwell.

3. 9/24/1851. Deed for sale of Atascadero by Samuel W. Haight to Henry Haight for $5,500.

4. 7/15/1853. Subscription for San Joaquin **Republican.**

5. 12/28/1854. Letter from James D. Thornton to ? Murphy. Mentions the opinion of Chief Justice Murray (California) published in the San Francisco **Herald** Dec. 28, 1854: ". . . Sacramento had been held to be the capital of the State."

6. Aug. 3, 1857. Sale of cattle for $2,417 to Henry Miller.

7. June 27, 1855. Note signed by R. P. Smith acknowledging payment for his building of St. Martin's Church, Gilroy.

8. Jan. 31, 1856. Note for $200 for fruit trees purchased by Daniel Murphy from J. W. Smith.

9. March 30, 1857. List of subscribers for building new church in Santa Cruz. (5 Murphys)

10. Bay View, Nov. 19, 1860. Note signed by Francisco Arce. Borrowed $200 from M. M. @ 2%.

11. July 27, 1861. Right of Way on Pastoria de las Borregas granted to San Francisco and San Jose R.R.

12. Oct. 1, 1870. Payment of $2,000 by Murphy for Lawrence Station on the S.F. and S.J. Railroad.

13. July 17, 1874. Subscription to "Irish Nationalist" by M. M. $6.00 per year. "The only Irish Nationalist Journal on the Pacific Coast."

14. Sept. 23, 1879. Deed of Sale of 149 A. of San Luis Obispo County to Murphy. Document signed by President Hayes; Land Act of 1820.

15. May 26, 1880. Receipt from Archbishop Alemany for $200 for Masses.

Partial list of letters sent to Mr. and Mrs. Murphy on the occasion of their Golden Jubilee:

7/11/1881	Lake Tahoe	W. J. Doyle to Mrs. Carroll (daughter)
7/12/1881	San Francisco	John M. Burnett to Mrs. Carroll
7/12/1881	San Francisco	Archbishop Alemany to Mrs. Carroll
7/13/1881	San Francisco	Father A. Varsi, S.J. to Mrs. Carroll
7/15/1881	Sacramento	Governor George C. Perkins to P. W. Murphy
7/18/1881	San Francisco	William T. Wallace to Martin Murphy, Jr.
7/18/1881	Menlo Park	John T. Doyle to Mrs. Carroll

Other letters of interest:

1. 4/27/1855   J. A. Forbes to Dan Murphy (brother of Martin). This letter states that "The Archbishop is here as a witness."
2. 6/20/1862   John E. Kincaid to Martin Murphy, Jr. re cost of construction of buildings in San Jose; $14,750.
3. 12/15/1880   Sr. Mary Cornelia to Martin Murphy re the death of Sr. Loyola in Cincinnati.
4. 12/ 1/1892   John Canon Parker of Ferns, County Wexford, Ireland to P. W. Murphy. Canon Parker was a first cousin of Mrs. Murphy, Mary Bolger. He read the account of her death in The Monitor (San Francisco Archdiocesan paper).

Insurance policies:

1. 1,000 tons of wheat @ $20,000. Stored at Murphy Station. 9/30/1880
2. $1,000 security for the one-story frame building for stable and hay barn 80 x 76 on rancho at Mountain View. 6/27/1881
3. $850 on 200 A. of wheat 6/27/1881 (at Mountain View)
4. $5,000 on two-story brick building - City Market Hall - SW corner of Market and Eldorado, San Jose

Documents regarding Martin Murphy, Jr.

1. The certificate of his membership in the Society of California Pioneers to which he was elected in 1853.
2. Certificate of Martin Murphy's citizenship in the United States. Murphy had become a citizen of Mexico when he arrived in the Sacramento area.

APPENDIX 7

The Golden Wedding Celebration

On July 18, 1881 a wedding anniversary brought together at Bay View the many admirers of the Golden Jubilarians Mr. and Mrs. Martin Murphy, Jr. who were among the early builders of California.[1] Some special invitations were sent but to avoid unintentional oversights, a general invitation was extended to relatives, friends, and acquaintances throughout the state by a notice in the San Jose *Daily Mercury*. Publication of this article began on June 15, 1881.

Monday, July 18th, will be the fiftieth anniversary of the marriage of our fellow citizen Martin Murphy and his estimable wife. In view of this fact it was proposed by members of the family and friends, that this event should be observed by a gathering at the Murphy homestead of the relatives and intimate friends. Mr. Murphy learned of the proposed arrangement, and emphatically announced that he neither could nor would undertake to discriminate or select among his many prized friends, old and new throughout the county and state. That he did not expect to celebrate but one golden wedding, and proposed that this celebration should be worthy so exceptional an event. And those familiar with the open-handed hospitality of the Murphys know what that means. The old gentleman has constituted himself a committee of one upon invitations. No special invitations whatever will be issued, but he invites everybody — all his old and new friends — to meet him at the Murphy homestead, Mountain View. On this golden anniversary — no presents expected or accepted. All that he wishes is to see all of his old friends around him on this occasion.[2]

On Monday, July 18th, the San Jose pioneer merchants declared a holiday; the banks closed at noon.[3]

The Board of Supervisors adjourned their meeting to attend and the jury, witnesses, and counsel of a Superior Court trial were freed for the afternoon by the judge who wanted to join in the festivities and decided that all might as well go with him.[4]

The Oak Grove Bay View ranch was the scene of the "greatest social event in Santa Clara County."[5] By mid-morning the dusty El Camino Real was lined with vehicles of all descriptions — buggies, carry-alls, and well-worn farm wagons — bringing several hundred gaily attired guests. Parkman's eighteen-piece band met the three hundred arrivals on board the excursion train from San Francisco. A similar escort met the San Joseans when they arrived shortly before noon.[6]

One end of the Oak Grove was the scene of barbecue preparations. "It was estimated that there were over three thousand people" on the grounds; the quantity of food provided for them was enormous.[7] The ditch for the barbecuing was over a hundred feet long and fired by seven cords of wood; veteran chef Uncle Ike Branham directed the corps of butchers, cooks, and carvers to prepare the seven beeves, fourteen sheep, and ten hogs.

For the next six hours while attendants turned the spits, the chef applied his famous and secretly prepared basting. As one account lyrically put it: 'With a small mop and a can of basting he moved from spit to spit and with the confidence of long experience, moistened the rich-smelling hides of the browning carcasses with the care that an artist applies the finishing touches of his exhibition painting.'[8]

John Gash, an architect, had been employed to construct an eighty by one-hundred-foot platform for dancing,[9] a stand for musicians, seats for spectators, and six tables seventy-five feet long where guests were seated a thousand at a time.[10]

At the opposite end of the grove under a canopy were seats for two made comfortable with cushions, robes, and decorative trimming. Suspended from the canopy was a large bell-shaped floral piece inset with the dates 1831-1881 presented by the San Franciscans.

The Murphys were serenaded at their home and then escorted to the bridal table on the platform while the band played "Come Haste to the Wedding."[12] An observant guest reported:

> When Mr. Murphy led his wife to the flower-filled table it was the signal for the general 'falling to' and the ladies speedily filled their seats while their escorts performed the pleasing task of looking over their shoulders and seeing that their dietary wants were well supplied from the abundant provisions on hand.[13]

Throughout the afternoon the thousands of guests were served. No formal program had been planned but numerous complimentary toasts were proposed to the Jubilarians so long identified with the progress and welfare of the state.[14] Among the speakers were such pioneer Californians as former United States Senator Gwin, Industrialist Colonel Peter Donahue of San Francisco, Tiburcio Parrot, Judge C. T. Ryland, and Martin Murphy's son General Patrick W. Murphy. Mr. Ryland's speech included words of praise for Mrs. Murphy; his tribute to her brought a standing ovation.[15] Poems celebrating the Golden Anniversary were read by the Murphy's sons, and by one of the twenty-two grandchildren present. Feasting, gaiety, and compliments continued as the well-wishers shared the hospitality and happiness of their hosts. After nightfall the merriment continued around the dance hall aglow with Chinese lanterns. "All passed off in baronial style and the Murphy Golden wedding will long be remembered."[16]

The following letters to Mr. and Mrs. Murphy on the occasion of their Jubilee are of particular interest.[17]

1. From Archbishop Alemany:
2. From Governor Perkins:
3. From William T. Wallace, a friend of Murphy's who drew up the deed of purchase for Pastoria de las Borregas in 1850:

1   Sacramento **Daily Bee**, Oct. 22, 1884.
2   San Jose **Daily Mercury**. Daily publication started on June 15, 1881. Acknowledgments received in Murphy Papers.

3 San Francisco **Alta California,** "A Pioneer's Golden Wedding," in column entitled "Sparks from the Wires," July 19, 1881.

4 San Francisco **Chronicle,** "Riptides," by Robert O'Brien, April 2, 1947.

5 San Francisco **Alta California,** July 19, 1881.

6 "Nearly all the notables of San Francisco and this county were present." **Ibid.**

7 ". . . a wagon load of hams, head cheese, bolognas, roasting chickens innumerable, salad served in bushel baskets, together with a sufficiency of bread, cake, and the necessary condiments. Guests downed the feast with five hundred gallons of coffee, fifteen barrels of lager beer from Krumb's, hogsheads of lemonade, and a freight car of choice vintages of France and California." San Francisco **Chronicle,** April 2, 1947.

8 **Ibid.**

9 The material used in this platform was afterwards donated by Murphy to the priests who used it to construct the first Mission chapel in Mountain View.

10 San Francisco **Chronicle,** April 2, 1947.

11 San Jose **Pioneer,** July 23, 1881.

12 San Francisco **Chronicle,** April 2, 1947. On the table was a huge stuffed bear, symbol of the Forty-Niners; in front of it was an elaborate wedding cake. **Ibid.**

13 **Ibid.**

14 Bancroft, **Chronicles,** p. 49.

15 **Ibid.,** p. 50.

16 San Francisco **Alta California,** July 19, 1881.

17 Original letters among Murphy Papers.

St. Mary's Cathedral
628 California St.
San Francisco, July 12, 1881

Dear in Christ Madam,

I am very thankful for the kind invitation you sent me to attend my dear old Friend's—your dearest parents' Golden Wedding. I will avail myself of the invitation and be present, at least in spirit, for I may be then moving 50 miles north to baptize a new Church. Anyway, I will humbly pray that God may grant them another Golden Wedding, if not in Mountain View, on the Mountain itself of heaven with two other Martins—Father and Son—and good Father DeVos, waiting the company of their children and grandchildren, who will no doubt follow the good example which has been set before them.

And may the mutual love of fifty years

Pledge them the Golden Land that knows no tears.

Yours Respectfully
+ J. S. Alemany. A.S.F.

Mrs. R. T. Carroll

State of California
Executive Department
Sacramento, Cal.
July 15, 1881

Hon. P. W. Murphy

My Dear Sir. I am today in receipt of your valued favor inviting me to a picnic—at Mountain View—on your Father's ranch on Monday 18th inst. the event being the celebration of your good Fathers golden wedding. In reply I would beg to say that I regret exceedingly that a previous engagement prevents me from being present. Please extend to your good people **my most hearty congratulations;** and, I trust the **event** will prove one of **much joy** and **pleasure** to all; and, **may every** member of your family **long live** to **enjoy** the **love** and **companionship** of **each other** is the **earnest** wish of

Sincerely Yours Geo. C. Perkins

San Francisco
July 18, 1881

Mr. Martin Murphy
Bay View

My dear friend,

I thank you most sincerely for your kind invitation to attend the celebration, this day, of the **fiftieth** anniversary of your marriage and am very sorry that my engagements here, in a cause actually on trial, prevent my presence with you upon the happy occasion.

Half a century of conjugal happiness is a boon vouchsafed by Providence to few indeed. Your personal career has been long and eventful and the fifty years of time to which this occasion points has been marked by greater human progress than the hundred which preceded. You and yours have borne an honorable and distinguished part in founding and building up the greatest one of the States which mark the western boundary of the Republic and your name is prominently associated with its wonderful progress to its present prosperous condition.

Though you have already passed the three score and ten years which the Psalmist numbers your age is clear as the noon-day.

Your children and your children's children, rise up and call you blessed but you still shine forth as the morning.

When last I had the pleasure of seeing you your appearance was about what it was when I first met you—thirty years ago. You have been wonderfully preserved. The sear and yellow leaf have not blighted your way of life and the honor, love, obedience, and troops of friends which should accompany old age are yours.

Long may you be spared to enjoy them all.

Your friend
Wm T. Wallace

APPENDIX 8

Martin Murphy's Last Will

Martin Murphy drew up his Will in 1883. True to his policy of running no unnecessary business or legal risks, he and his wife divided their property equally among their heirs, designating what land each was to have and thereby avoiding all expense of probate and partition,[1] and making joint deeds of trust for the holding of their property until the death of him who had accumulated it.[2]

Mrs. Murphy retains a life interest in an ample sufficiency of the personal property to meet her every want, while the remainder goes to the heirs without the intervention of administrators or executors and without the dangers that always attend the settling of large properties by will. The estate has been divided into six equal portions which have been given as follows: A share each to the five children of the deceased, viz.: Senator Patrick W. Murphy of San Luis Obispo; Senator Bernard D. Murphy of Santa Clara; Hon. James T. Murphy, ex-bank Commissioner and elector on the Cleveland ticket; Mrs. Richard T. Carroll; and the widow of J. R. Arques. The sixth portion goes to the four orphan children of Mr. and Mrs. William P. Taaffe, the latter having been a daughter of the deceased.[3]

His sons received the large ranches in the San Luis Obispo County and the subdivided Mountain View tract of Pastoria de las Borregas (Bay View). His daughters received ownership of the real estate in the city of San Jose. A sixth portion was given to William, Martin, Matilda, and Mary E. Taaffe, the four children of the deceased Mr. and Mrs. William P. Taaffe (Elizabeth Yuba).[4]

Shortly after Mr. Murphy's death the subdivision of the property excited considerable interest. In connection with the details stated above, it is interesting to recall contemporary estimates of the value of these holdings as reflected in published accounts. The following facts were published by the San Francisco *Morning Call*:

The property thus divided is stated, by those who know its every item, to have a market value of considerably over $3,000,000. The realty consists of 10,000 acres in Santa Barbara County, 12,000 acres in Santa Clara County, 60,000 acres in San Luis Obispo County, a large amount of improved and unimproved property in San Jose and about $100,000 worth of real estate in San Francisco. As Mr. Murphy never invested in railroad or mining stock, the personal property is confined to bank stocks, water company stocks, and mortgages.[5]

An article in the Sacramento *Daily Bee* gave $5,000,000 as the estimated value of the estate.[6] *The Wave* described this amount as excessive and quoted the value of all lands and cattle to be worth $3,000,000.[7]

The San Luis Obispo ranchos of 110,000 acres were described as "a principality" extending for fifty miles along the base of the Coast Range mountains Though much of this territory was useful only for cattle grazing, Santa Margarita came into the railroad picture in 1889 when part of the rancho was subdivided and the land auctioned off in order to promote the new town. Referring to the future value of this property, *The Wave* article continued: "In the course of time when the overland line is finished from Templeton through to Santa Barbara, this will indeed be valuable land."[8] By 1894 the Southern Pacific route had reached San Luis Obispo, and by 1901 Guadalupe on the shore line of Santa Barbara County.[9] "No longer would visitors, settlers, merchants, and traders have to depend on stage coaches or steamer landings" to reach this vast interior area of central California. The great development of San Luis Obispo County and consequent rise of property values in that area stem from the building of the Southern Pacific Railroad.[10]

The park-like area of Pastoria de las Borregas Rancho was subdivided into 500-acre tracts but "from the Mountain View ranch a very large income is not derived though it is really the most valuable property of the estate."[11] One of the sections owned later by the City of Sunnyvale remained the site of the historic Murphy house until its demolition in 1961 (Appendix 2).

In 1892, an article in *The Wave* described the San Jose city property in the following summary statement explaining its devaluation:

The San Jose property is no longer valuable as in days of yore. More enterprising capitalists have built in a different part of town, structures of modern style, whose existence has diverted the center of trade from the Murphy holding, which is covered with obsolete buildings that rent for a tithe of what they used to bring in.[12]

The revenues from all these property holdings formed a common fund which Bernard D. Murphy administered. Each member of the family received an allowance and the surplus was invested according to his judgment. Contemporary opinion estimated these revenues to be considerably less than what was "ordinarily supposed":

Considering the vast holdings of the family and the amount of coin they represent, the revenue is by no means as great as is ordinarily supposed. Indeed rumor has it as $60,000—surely a meager return for $5,000,000 invested. Now, however, that the individual members of the family have their own property, perhaps they will take measure to compel it to yield a larger income. I doubt if they will reverse the family tradition and dispose of the rood of the land.[13]

The text of Murphy's last Will follows:[14]

Martin Murphy

In the name of God. Amen.

I, Martin Murphy, of the county of Santa Clara, being at present of sound mind and disposing memory but infirm in health and mindful of the uncertainties of life, have and I do hereby make publish and declare this my Last Will and Testament

1. I hereby direct that all my just debts and funeral expenses be paid.
2. I hereby give, devise and bequeath all my property of every name, nature of description and whatever situate unto my beloved wife Mary Murphy.
3. I do not herein provide for any of my children or grandchildren for the reason that I have heretofore made ample provision for them and at the same time well knowing that their mother will make such provision as in her judgment shall be best for their interests.
4. I hereby revoke any and all wills that I may at any time heretofore have made.
5. I hereby nominate and appoint my beloved wife Mary Murphy executrix and my sons Patrick W., Bernard D., executors of this my last will and expressly declare that no bond or undertaking of any nature or description shall be exacted of them in performance of any of their duties as such executrix and executors under this my last will

In witness of all which I have hereunto set my hand and seal this tenth day of February A. D. 1883

his
Martin (X) Murphy
mark

1 "The peculiarity of my father's distribution was that he and my mother, when the old gentleman found that he had not much longer to live, joined in a deed distributing the property equally among all the children, sons and daughters share and share alike, simply reserving a life interest of the rents and profits. In that way all the expense of probate and partition were avoided, as he designated the land each should occupy." Murphy Dictation, p. 11.
2 San Francisco **Morning Call,** Oct. 21, 1884.
3 **Ibid.**
4 "Subdivision of Estate," **The Wave,** Vol. 9, No. 12, Sept. 17, 1892.
5 San Francisco **Morning Call,** Oct. 21, 1884.
6 Sacramento **Daily Bee,** Oct. 22, 1884.
7 **The Wave,** Sept. 17, 1892.
8 **Ibid.**
9 **The Story of San Luis Obispo County** (Los Angeles: Title Insurance and Trust Company, 1965), p. 31.
10 **Ibid.**
11 **The Wave,** Sept. 17, 1892.
12 **Ibid.**
13 **Ibid.** "It was said of Martin Murphy that no one had ever seen his signature to either a deed or a mortgage. He bought but he never sold."
14 **Will Roll Book F,** Probate Department, Superior Court, Santa Clara County. "Last Wills and Testaments of Santa Clara County," p. 129.

I PRIMARY SOURCES

A. Unpublished Primary Material

"Alemany Journal of Correspondence," Vol. H 15. Archives of the Archdiocese of San Francisco in Chancery Office, San Francisco.

Bates, Alfred. "Martin Murphy. Dictation given by Hon. B. D. Murphy of San Jose." MS, Bancroft Library, University of California, Berkeley.

Hambly, Harry B. "List of Subscribers to **Chronicles of the Builders of the Commonwealth.**" MS, Bancroft Library, University of California, Berkeley.

"Historical Documents of California," Vol. III, Bancroft Library, University of California, Berkeley.

McQuoid, William R. "Letter to Hubert Howe Bancroft." MS, Bancroft Library, University of California, Berkeley.

"Murphy Family Chronology." Murphy Papers. College of Notre Dame, Belmont, California.

"Murphy Papers: Letters and Business Transactions." College of Notre Dame, Belmont, California.

"Poll Lists of the Election Districts of the County of Santa Clara 1867-1879." San Jose, 1871.

"Register for the Society of California Pioneers." California Pioneer Society, San Francisco.

"Will Roll Call Book F." Probate Department, Superior Court, Santa Clara, California.

B. Printed Source Material

Bidwell, John. **Echoes of the Past About California.** Edited by Milo Quaife. Chicago: Lakeside Press, 1928.

Burnett, P. H. **Recollections and Opinions of an Old Pioneer.** New York: Appleton and Co., 1880

Census Reports 1870, 1880. U. S. Federal Census. Washington, D.C.: Government Printing Office.

Dana, R. H. **Two Years Before the Mast.** New York: Random House, 1936.

Davis, W. H. **60 Years in California 1831-1889.** San Francisco: A. J. Leary, 1889.

Gates, M. J. **Pastoria de las Borregas, Mountain View, California.** San Francisco: Cottle and Murgotten, 1895.

Hewson, J. B., ed. **Directory of the City of San Jose for 1874.** San Francisco: Bacon and Co., 1874.

Larkin, Thomas O. **Larkin Papers.** Edited by George P. Hammond. Vol. V (1846). 7 vols. Berkeley: University of California Press, 1955.

Sherman, William T. **Memoirs.** Vol. I. New York: D. Appleton and Co., 1875.

Sutter, John A. **New Helvetia Diary.** San Francisco: The Grabhorn Press, 1939.

Taylor, James Bayard. **Eldorado or Adventures in the Path of Empire.** New York: G. P. Putnam's Sons, 1850.

II SECONDARY MATERIAL

A. Unpublished Material

Conmy, Peter T. "Stevens-Murphy Party of 1844." Grand Historian, Native Sons of the Golden West, November 1, 1942. Mimeographed copy in Bancroft Library, University of California, Berkeley.

Corbett, Francis. "Primer on the California Land Grants." Typed copy, College of Notre Dame, Belmont, California.

Gray, Sister Gertrude Mary. "A Preliminary Survey of the Life of the Most Reverend Joseph Sadoc Alemany, O.P., First Archbishop of San Francisco." Unpublished Master's thesis, Catholic University of America, 1943.

Murphy, Cecilia M. "The Stevens-Murphy Overland Party of 1844." Unpublished Master's thesis, University of California, 1941.

B. Printed Material

Adams, William F. **Ireland and Irish Emigration to the New World from 1815 to the Famine.** New Haven: Yale University Press, 1932.

Angel, Myron. **History of San Luis Obispo County.** San Francisco: Thompson and West, 1883.

Annals of San Francisco. Edited by Frank Soule **et al.** New York: D. Appleton and Co., 1855.

Bancroft, H. H. **Chronicles of the Builders of the Commonwealth.** Vol. III. San Francisco: The History Co., 1891.

———. **History of California.** 7 vols. San Francisco: The History Co., 1891.

Bechdolt, F. R. **Giants of the Old West.** New York: The Century Co., 1930.

Brebner, J. B. **Canada: A History.** Ann Arbor: University of Michigan Press, 1960.

Caughey, J. W. **California.** New York: Prentice-Hall, Inc., 1940.

———. **H. H. Bancroft.** Berkeley: University of California Press, 1946.

Centennial Book, 1865-1965. Edited by Charles E. Pillman. Gilroy, California: Dispatch Printing, 1965.

Chauvire, Roger. **A Short History of Ireland.** New York: The Devin-Adair Co., 1956.

Chittenden, H. M. **The American Fur Trade of the Far West.** 2 vols. Stanford: Academic Reprints, 1954.

Cleland, R. G. **From Wilderness to Empire: A History of California.** New York: Alfred Knopf, 1959.

———. **A History of California: The American Period.** New York: The Macmillan Co., 1939.

Davis, J. F. **California: Romantic and Resourceful.** San Francisco: A. M. Robertson, 1914.

Dunn, Joseph, ed. **The Glories of Ireland.** Washington, D.C.: Phoenix Limited, 1914.

Ellison, Joseph. **California and the Nation 1850-1869.** Berkeley: University of California Press, 1927.

Evans, E. E. **Irish Heritage: The Landscape, The People and Their Work.** Dundalk W. Tempest: Dundalgan Press, 1949.

Foote, H. S. **Pen Pictures of Santa Clara County.** Chicago: The Lewis Publishing Co., 1888.

Frost, John. **History of the State of California.** New York: Hurst and Co., 1859.

Guinn, J. M. **A History of the State of California.** Chicago: Chapman Publishing Co., 1904.

Hall, Frederick. **History of San Jose.** San Francisco: A. L. Bancroft and Co., 1871.

Hanna, P. T. **California Through Four Centuries.** New York: Farrar and Rinehart, 1935.

Hoover, Mildred Brooke. **Historic Spots in California.** Stanford: Stanford University Press, 1966. Reprint.

Hunt, R. D. **California and Californians.** 4 vols. San Francisco: The Lewis Publishing Co., 1930.

———. **California Firsts.** G. F. Fearon Pub., 1957.

———. "California in Review After a Century of American Control," **Centennial Lectures.** Washington, D.C.: Government Printing Office, 1948.

———. **John Bidwell, Prince of California Pioneers.** Caldwell, Idaho: The Caxton Printers, 1942.

James, William F., and George H. McMurry. **History of San Jose.** San Jose: A. H. Cawston Publishers, 1933.

Jones, Maldwyn Allen. **American Immigration. Chicago:** University of Chicago Press, 1960.

Joyce, P. W. **The Origin and History of Irish Names and Places.** New York: Longmans, Green and Co., 1901.

Latta, Frank F. "Alexis Godey in Kern County." Kern County Historical Society, V. Bakersfield, California, November, 1939.

Laveille, E., S.J. **The Life of Father De Smet, S.J.** New York: P. J. Kenedy and Sons, 1915.

Lecky, William. **History of Ireland.** Vol. I. London: Longmans, Green and Co., 1913.

Marmion, Anthony. **The Ancient and Modern History of the Maritime Ports of Ireland.** London: W. H. Cox, 1858.

McInnis, Edgar. **Canada: a Political and Social History.** New York: Rinehart and Co., 1959.

McNamee, Sister Mary Dominica. **Willamette Interlude.** Palo Alto, California: Pacific Books, 1959.

Millard, Frank B. **History of the San Francisco Bay Region.** San Francisco: The American Historical Society, 1924.

Munro-Fraser, J. P. **History of Santa Clara County.** San Francisco: Alley, Bowen and Co., 1881.

Norton, Henry K. **The Story of California.** Chicago: A. C. McClurg and Co., 1924.

O'Connor, James. **History of Ireland.** London: Edward Arnold, 1925.

Official Guide to County Wexford. Published by Wexford Chamber of Commerce, Wexford, Ireland, n.d.

Quigley, Hugh. **The Irish Race in California and on the Pacific Coast.** San Francisco: A. Roman and Co., 1878.

Rolle, A. F. **California.** New York: Thomas Y. Crowell Co., 1963.

Royce, Josiah. **California.** New York: Alfred Knopf, 1948.

Sawyer, Eugene T. **History of Santa Clara County.** Los Angeles: Historic Record Co., 1922.

Stewart, George R. **The California Trail.** New York: McGraw-Hill Book Co., 1962.

———. **The Opening of the California Trail.** Berkeley: University of California Press, 1953.

Story of San Luis Obispo County. Los Angeles: Title Insurance and Trust Co., 1957.

Sunnyvale Historical Society Program for the Erection of California Landmark No. 644, May. 1960, Sunnyvale Historical Society.

University of Santa Clara; A History. Santa Clara: University of Santa Clara Press, 1912.

West, Mary. **Sunnyvale Historical Society Bulletin.** August, 1959. (Mimeographed.)

Young, Edward. **Special Report on Immigration.** Philadelphia: M'Laughlin Brothers, 1871.

III ORAL AND WRITTEN TESTIMONY

Interview with Miss Muriel Wright, great-granddaughter of Martin Murphy, Jr., San Jose, November 29, 1968.

Letters from:

Mrs. Frank R. Stockton, great-granddaughter of Murphy, June 5, 1968.

Mrs. Robert C. Tipton, great-granddaughter of Murphy, July, 1965.

Reverend William Schoenberg, S.J., concerning the Fathers Christian and Adrian Hoecken, S.J. March 16, 1964.

IV ARTICLES AND PERIODICALS

[Fitzgerald, Marcella A.]. "Irish Pioneers of California: Martin Murphy, Sr." The Monitor, LIII, No. 21 (August 24, 1901).

Ghent, W. G. "Christopher Carson." Dictionary of American Biographies. New York: Scribners' Sons, 1936.

Hawgood, John A. "The Pattern of Yankee Infiltration in Mexican Alta California 1821-1846." **Pacific Historical Review,** XXVII (February, 1958),

"In Memoriam." **California Historical Quarterly,** XXV (March, 1954), 88.

Nevins, Allan. "John Charles Fremont," Dictionary of American Biographies. New York: Scribner's Sons, 1936.

Price, Glenn. "Murphy's Ranch - New State Landmark." **The Pacific Historian** (May, 1959), p. 30.

Sears, L. M. "Thomas Hart Benton." Dictionary of American Biographies. New York: Scribner's Sons, 1936.

"Squatter Riot of '50 in Sacramento." **Overland Monthly,** ser. 2, VI (September, 1855), 225-246.

"Subdivision of Estate." **The Wave,** IX, No. 12 (September 17, 1892).

Wright, Doris M. "The Making of Cosmopolitan California 1848-1870." **California Historical Quarterly,** XIX-XX (December, 1940-March, 1941), 323-343; 65-79.

V NEWSPAPERS

Oakland:

Tribune, April 24, 1960.

Sacramento:

Daily Bee, Oct. 22, 1884.

Union, Oct. 21, 1884; Aug. 30, 1892.

San Francisco:

Alta California, Jan. 11, 1849; June, 1865 to 1881.

Chronicle, March, April, 1947.

Morning Call, Oct. 21, 1884; August, September, 1892.

San Jose:

Pioneer, April to July, 1880.

Daily Mercury, June 15, 1881.

Pioneer, July to November, 1881; Jan. 14, 1893.

Mercury, June 17, 1951; Jan. 13, 1954.

Evening News, May 23, 1960.

Sunnyvale:

Daily Standard, Dec. 26, 1961.

DATE DUE